"How fine that Fr. Rutler's wit and learning
are now reaching another audience."
—*William F. Buckley Jr.*

"An important, fascinating author."
—*John Cardinal O'Connor*

"The author's works are often unusual in their insights,
their range of knowledge, and the elegance of the writing."
—*George Cardinal Pell*

"Fr. Rutler offers clarity, hope, and purpose."
—*Laura Ingraham*

"An accomplished man of letters who
writes as gracefully as he speaks."
—*George Weigel*

"There is no other writer in the world like Fr. George Rutler."
—*Anthony Esolen*

"A penetrating seriousness, with a mind informed
by the ages, in the best things said and done."
—*Hadley Arkes*

A Year *with* Father Rutler

George William Rutler

A Year with Father Rutler

Pentecost and Summer

VOLUME 3

Edited by Duncan Maxwell Anderson

SOPHIA INSTITUTE PRESS
Manchester, New Hampshire

This book is a selection of Father George Rutler's columns from his weekly parish bulletins dated 2001 to 2017.

Cover and interior design by Perceptions Design Studio.

Sophia Institute Press
Box 5284, Manchester, NH 03108
1-800-888-9344

www.SophiaInstitute.com

2017 edition

Library of Congress Cataloging-in-Publication Data

Names: Rutler, George W. (George William), author.
Title: A year with Father Rutler : a pastor speaks to his people / George William Rutler ; edited by Duncan Maxwell Anderson.
Description: Manchester, New Hampshire : Sophia Institute Press, 2017. | Includes bibliographical references.
Identifiers: LCCN 2017024886 | ISBN 9781622823840 (leatherbound : alk. paper)
Subjects: LCSH: Church year meditations. | History, Modern — 21st century — Miscellanea.
Classification: LCC BX2170.C55 R884 2017 | DDC 242/.3 — dc23 LC record available at https://lccn.loc.gov/2017024886

2019 edition
978-1-64413-266-1 (vol. 1)
978-1-64413-269-2 (vol. 2)
978-1-64413-272-2 (vol. 3)
978-1-64413-275-3 (vol. 4)
978-1-64413-278-4 (4-volume set)

Library of Congress Control Number:2019954891

First printing

The publication of *A Year with Father Rutler*
was made possible through the generosity of:

Sean Fieler
Joseph J. Frank
William Grace
Mr. and Mrs. Vincenzo La Ruffa
Mr. And Mrs. Arthur S. Long

Contents

Pentecost

The Blessed Trinity

The Body and Blood of Christ

The Sacred Heart of Jesus

Pentecost

The Gifts of Fire and Fortitude

Truth

On the fiftieth day after the Resurrection, God filled His Church with the Holy Spirit. Jesus kept His promise: "When the Spirit of truth comes, he will guide you into all truth" (John 16:13). Pentecost is the start of Christian life, rather than the end of the story, rather as Churchill said after the Battle of El Alamein: "Now this is not the end. It is not even the beginning of the end. But it is, perhaps, the end of the beginning."[1]

The power the Holy Spirit gives the Church is the truth. Truth is the ultimate power because it is reality. "Men may all lie, but God is always true" (Rom. 3:4). Truth always wins in the long run. In the short run, it may seem that lies win. But truth sustains life while falsehood destroys it. Jesus said that Satan "was a murderer from the beginning, and does not stand in the truth, because there is no truth in him. Whenever he speaks a lie, he speaks from his own nature; for he is a liar, and the father of lies" (John 8:44). Lies do have power, but it is a fatal power and eventually self-destructs. In our society there are lies that an unborn baby is not human, and that marriage is not naturally the union of male and female, and that truth is only opinion. When a society accepts these lies, it eventually clashes with inescapable reality and crumbles. Even Satan is forced to tell the truth in the presence of Christ: "I know who you are, the Holy One of God" (Mark 1:24).

[1] Winston Churchill, "The End of the Beginning" (speech at the Mansion House, London, November 10, 1942).

A recent film, *Angels and Demons*, is the latest embarrassing attempt to lie about Christ and His Church. It is filled with amateurish technical mistakes, not to mention the historical and archeological ones. The script says the Church opposes scientific truth, when in fact, as the recently deceased Benedictine priest Stanley Jaki explained in dozens of books, the Church provides the philosophical matrix for the motive and method of physical science. The Church attends to the truths of Heaven, but she does not neglect physical science, because God made the world as a blessing.

Galileo, whom the film mentions as a member of an esoteric secularist sect known as the Illuminati (which, in fact, was founded two centuries after Galileo), became the leading member of the original Pontifical Academy of Sciences founded under the patronage of Pope Clement VIII. Major discoveries in mathematics, astronomy, physics, genetics, botany, zoology, and medicine have taken place in universities established by the Church, and they continue to be the work of Catholics from John XXI and Sylvester II, through Hermann of Reichenau, Robert Grosseteste, Roger Bacon, Albertus Magnus, Jean Buridan, René Descartes, Nicolaus Copernicus, Anton Schyrleus, Blaise Pascal, Juan Caramuel y Lobkowitz, Angelo Secchi, Louis Pasteur, Alexis Carrel, Guglielmo Marconi, Alexander Fleming, up to Father Georges Lemaître, who proposed the Big Bang theory.

On Pentecost and during the week following, we rejoice that "God cannot lie" (Titus 1:2). The same cannot be said of Hollywood.

May 31, 2009

Tongues of Fire

St. Peter preached a most powerful sermon on this day in Jerusalem and baptized thousands: proof of the Holy Spirit at work, since Peter would be the first to admit that he was worthless without that supernatural help.

That is history, but we are making history in these days in a most spectacular way. The holy death of Pope John Paul II woke many people up to the mystery of suffering and dying, and the choice of Joseph Ratzinger as Pope is an inspired evidence of God at work. How vain are those remote pundits who disdain the gospel and say that the Church is out of touch. The Church is God's instrument for touching His Holy Face. Millions of young people prayed at the late Pope's funeral and rejoiced in his promised glory, and days later they and countless faithful throughout the world marveled at what God had done in giving us Benedict XVI. Our celebration of Pentecost is a little late this year: in terms of the calendar, it is unusually early, but it comes after so many marvelous workings of the Holy Spirit. Holy Week and Easter with the death of a Pope and the appearance of another Pope, and the mystical configuration of the liturgical readings for all those days, as if we were living in the first days of the Acts of the Apostles, made us part of the first Pentecost, when the crowds were converted by the preaching of Peter and his fellow apostles.

We live in times when our almighty God is especially vivid and dramatically active. This may be due to Our Lord's decision that our faithless generation needs signs and wonders for our unbelief. Nonetheless, the signs are there, and we are accountable to Him for accepting or rejecting them. To do His work on earth, the Holy Spirit gives us the seven gifts of wisdom, understanding, knowledge, counsel, piety, fortitude, and fear of the Lord. You can read about them on websites[2] or read about them in the *Catechism*. But the reading is frail prelude to the living of them.

Each week, we have a goodly number of new people worshipping in our parish. Do find ways to introduce yourselves to our new parishioners, and also pray for the children receiving the sacraments of Confession and Holy Eucharist in these bright days of May. Offer your own Communions and confessions for our new Holy Father, Pope Benedict XVI, who has great works to do for us and with us in the power of the Holy Spirit.

May 15, 2005

[2] At NewAdvent.org, for instance—search for "Holy Spirit, gifts."

Citizens of Heaven

Religions contrived merely by humans tend to be exotic. But in the only actual instance of perfect divinity and perfect humanity united in a historical figure, Christ does not go about dressed as a wizard, and He tries to keep His miracles confidential: "Tell no one" (see, e.g., Matt. 8:4). He makes all things new (Rev. 21:5), but He does not make new things. Thus, Aquinas wrote: "Grace does not destroy nature, but perfects it."[3]

In the Resurrection, the Lord goes to lengths to show that He is not a ghost, even to eating familiar food. In the Ascension, when He vanishes into what limited language could best describe as a cloud, two men in white soberly ask those whose mouths are agape: "Why are you standing there, looking at the sky?" (Acts 1:11). For God—whose utterance "Let there be light" came billions of years before there was anyone to hear it—the Incarnation was, from the perspective of eternity, a holy mystery and not an artificial mystification.

On Pentecost, the apostles are not changed physically. They are changed into moral agents of God's power. Peter will have to tell Cornelius not to kneel before him because "I am only a man" (Acts 10:26). Paul and Barnabas will have to disabuse the pagan priest and people of Lystra (in what now is Turkey) of the conceit that they are Hermes and Zeus (Acts 14:12–13). A few years before, no one in Capernaum thought that Peter was anything but a fisherman, and a year back no one wanted to sacrifice garlanded oxen to Paul and Barnabas.

[3] St. Thomas Aquinas, *Summa Theologica*, I, Q. 1, art. 8.

Little more than a century after all this, an anonymous writer tried to explain Christians to a man named Diognetus. In one passage he says, "They do not inhabit cities of their own, use a particular way of speaking, or lead a life marked by any curiosity." They marry and have children like everyone else, but they do not destroy their offspring, and they share their food, but not their spouses. It is in their ordinary way of life "that they display to us their wonderful and admittedly striking way of life." For Christians, "every foreign land is like a homeland to them, and every land of their birth is like a land of strangers." Here is grace at work on their nature: "They exist in the flesh, but they do not live by the flesh. They pass their days on earth, but they are citizens of heaven."

Stripped of its modern inventions, our culture is very like that in the fresh wake of Pentecost. Human nature is always the same, but grace can transform it without destroying it. Christians today, as back then, "are spoken ill of and yet are justified." And as Diognetus learned, those who hate them "are unable to give any reason for their hatred."

May 17, 2015

Instruments of God

The fire that Moses saw was not by any definition what we know as fire, for it did not burn the blazing bush. The light that shone from Christ in His Transfiguration was not what is light in the canons of natural physics, because it was of an intensity beyond accessible description—without damaging the sight of Peter, James, and John. Fifty days after the Resurrection, in the Upper Room, there was a noise "like" a driving wind, and then flames "as of" fire shone over the heads of the apostles. The description required similitudes because the noise and the flames were not a natural noise and fire.

Christ promised that the Holy Spirit would enable human intelligence to embrace depths of reality beyond the limits of natural experience. Here at work is a principle of St. Thomas Aquinas: "Grace does not destroy nature, but perfects it." The apostles became more intensely human when they received the power of the Holy Spirit: they traveled to lands beyond the limited environs of their early years, with a courage never before tested. They received the "glory" that Christ, on the night before He died, prayed that His disciples might share. Because that participation in the divine nature bridges time and eternity, there is an invigorating terror about it—not the dread of being diminished or annihilated, but the trembling awesomeness of breaking the bonds of death itself.

When the Holy Spirit moves a man from aimless biological existence to what Christ calls the "fullness" of life, the reaction is a little like that of someone who has heard simple tunes but then encounters a symphony. Simple pleasure may evoke smiles and then laughter, but the deepest joy can move one to tears, and that is why there is that curious experience not of laughing for joy, but weeping for joy, and the equally enigmatic experience of lovesickness.

Oft quoted is the diary account by Samuel Pepys in the seventeenth century after attending a concert: "That which did please me beyond anything in the whole world was the wind-musique when the Angel comes down, which is so sweet that it ravished me; and endeed, in a word, did wrap up my soul so that it made me really sick, just as I have formerly been when in love with my wife."

A fan of Jascha Heifetz told him after a performance that his violin had such a beautiful tone. The maestro placed his ear against the Stradivarius and said, "I hear nothing."

By way of metaphor, it may be said that we exist biologically as wonderful instruments: the brain itself is the most complex organism in the universe. But we make celestial music only when the Holy Spirit conjoins our human nature with the Source of Life.

June 4, 2017

The Power of the Holy Spirit

Arriving in Ephesus, in what now is Turkey, St. Paul encountered some twelve men who had news of the Resurrection but had not followed through on its consequences. So he asked them if they had received the Holy Spirit, to which they replied, "No, we were never even told that there was such a thing as a Holy Spirit" (Acts 19:2). The fact that they spoke of "a Holy Spirit" instead of "the Holy Spirit" let St. Paul know that he had his work cut out for him.

Those Ephesians were ignorant, which is not necessarily an insult. Unlike stupidity, which has no cure short of a brain transplant, ignorance can be cured by an injection of information. I know practically nothing about the inner workings of a computer, but I know a lot more about the history of the Saxon kings than the computer engineer who is patient when I have a problem with the Internet. Just as he does not think I am stupid for not knowing how to design a website, I do not belittle him for never having heard of the kings Aethelwald and Aethelberht. Together, resolving each other's ignorance, we might rebuild civilization. St. Paul dug in his heels and wiped away the ignorance of those Ephesians by baptizing them with the power of the Holy Spirit.

Pentecost and Easter are the central feasts of the Church. Without Easter there would be no Christianity, and without Pentecost there would be no Christians. Wherever the number of Christians increases, it is because of the Holy Spirit, and wherever they decline, it is because the Holy Spirit is absent. Polls now indicate that there is a vast number of "former Catholics." This surprises some who thought that bureaucratic programs, enhanced communications, or a new Pope would change things. To some degree, there have been positive influences: the number of men ordained to the priesthood in the United States, having been formed during the pontificate of Pope Benedict XVI, increased 25 percent in just one year. The indications now are of a downward slope. To rely on personalities is to "place your trust in princes," which the psalmist says is a bad policy (Ps. 118:9). Trust the Holy Spirit. He gives the gifts needed to change the world: wisdom, understanding, counsel, fortitude, knowledge, piety, and fear of the Lord.

Did I say that those who had never heard of the Holy Spirit were Ephesians? You can meet them anywhere: some are doctors, politicians, financial managers, retailers, soldiers, professors, and even highly placed clergymen. They may be ignorant, but they are not stupid. Willful ignorance covers ears at the mention of the Holy Spirit, and there is a moral accountability to be exacted for that. But there are many smart people who are not intentionally ignorant. An informed Christian is at fault if he does not instruct those who are ignorant by default.

May 24, 2015

Founded upon Humility

The Resurrection of Christ and the descent of the Holy Spirit brought the Church into being, and so Easter and Pentecost were the first two great feasts. On Pentecost the Holy Spirit gave the Church seven spiritual gifts, and these are given to each Christian in the sacrament of confirmation: wisdom, understanding, knowledge, counsel, piety, fortitude, and fear of the Lord. These are not altogether what they mean in ordinary speech, and it is good to read about them and to use the season of Pentecost to pray for their increase.

We can offer Communions and confessions for their increase, and this bears results. The baptisms in our parish have increased 30 percent over two years ago and are 80 percent more than twenty years ago. The increasing number of confessions creates a nice symmetry: the more confessions are offered for the good of others, the more others come to confession. Can you think of a better place for spreading God's grace than right here in our parish in the heart of Manhattan? This is a big responsibility: Our Lord told us that more is required from those to whom much is given.

The Holy Spirit leads into all truth. Pope John Paul II has called the loss of a sense of truth the greatest calamity of the age. When the Holy Spirit is driven from the soul by pride, the ego and its counterfeits for Catholic truth take over. "God wants this or that" becomes a falsely pious way of saying, "I want this or that." Bogus invocations of the Holy Spirit have led to a decrease in faith, with resulting sadness and moral chaos. There can be no true joy without the truth of God.

It is remarkable that there seems to be such an increase of faith in so many in a time of such confusion, but that is a paradox of the Holy

Spirit's mercy for us. Nonetheless, those who propose reforms for a decadent society will fail if they seek legal and political solutions without the help of the Holy Spirit. The media have exercised their proper office in demanding accountability for the moral failings of Christians. They have done poorly themselves. Our major city newspaper, not reluctant to find fault with the Church, has had major ethical scandals recently and has refused to fire its editors. Nor has it ever apologized for having defended characters such as Stalin and Castro, or for having cast a largely blind eye on the early reports of Nazi genocide. The list goes on.

Truth is not a theory, but a fact. It is not determined by opinion. It is found by humility. The ideologue says, "That may be fine in practice, but how is it in theory?" The Christian says, "Come Holy Spirit, enlighten our hearts, and kindle in them the fire of Thy love."

June 8, 2003

Fortitude

Among the seven Pentecostal gifts of the Holy Spirit with which we were "sealed" in the sacrament of Confirmation is fortitude. Fortitude is strength and power infused by God to help overcome difficulties or to endure pain. This "impulse of the Holy Spirit" perfects the natural virtue of courage so that it resists evil and perseveres toward eternal life. Its characteristics are energy, steadiness, promptness, and a confidence of success.

Over the Memorial Day weekend, I preached about Father Vincent Capodanno, a model of fortitude. He was born on February 13, 1929, on Staten Island, and the hardships of the Depression were vivid in his large family. After his priestly ordination in 1957 he spent eight years as a Maryknoll missioner in Taiwan and Hong Kong. A year after enlisting in the navy as a chaplain in 1965, he was assigned to Vietnam with the marines as a battalion chaplain, and his pastoral care for the marine infantrymen who were called "grunts" soon got him the nickname "the grunt padre." He requested that his one-year tour of duty in Vietnam be extended. On the front line in Que Son Valley, September 4, 1967, his men were outnumbered by the enemy 2,500 to 500. Early on, with two Purple Hearts already to his credit, he had part of his right hand blown away—but he continued to hear confessions and anoint the dying. A mortar shell left his right arm hanging in shreds, but he continued to give absolution, supporting what remained of that arm with his left one. When one of the soldiers was shot in the leg, he positioned himself between the wounded young man and the machine gun aimed at him. His body, with twenty-eight bullets, was carried off the field by troops to whom he had given Communion many times. Posthumously, Father Capodanno was awarded the Medal of Honor.

It is military tradition that anyone wearing the Medal of Honor, however low his rank, is saluted even by generals and the commander-in-chief. A higher salute awaits those who live the virtues heroically through the power of the Holy Spirit. This May 21 in Washington, DC, 1,500 people attended a Mass opening the cause for the possible canonization of this Servant of God. Father Louis Iasiello, a rear admiral and chief of navy chaplains, said Fr. Capodanno was "more than a person of extraordinary military accomplishment.... He was also a Christian who lived an exemplary life of extraordinary virtue ... who, through the testament of his life, offers all believers a model of faith to inspire them to live, more deeply, their own vocation."

St. Cyril of Jerusalem said that the Holy Spirit "apportions grace to each man as He wills.... He comes with the tenderness of a true friend and protector to save, to heal, to teach, to counsel, to strengthen, and to console."[4]

June 4, 2006

[4] St. Cyril of Jerusalem, *De Spiritu Sancto*.

The Upper Room

Our Lord had sent the apostles into Jerusalem to prepare the Passover meal with explicit instructions about finding an upper room owned by a certain man whom he described in detail. The apostles found everything just as the Master had said. The Gospel accounts of those extraordinary days leading up to and following the Crucifixion and Resurrection are full of details, such as the arrangement of the shroud and linen face covering in the empty tomb. That "room for rent" was transformed by the institution of the Eucharist and the appearance of the Risen Lord there, with the doors locked, on two Sundays. After the Ascension, that same room became an oratory where the apostles and Our Lady and others, some specifically named, waited for the coming of the Holy Spirit, as promised.

Our Lord never fails to keep His promises, and the rushing wind and the flames that settled on each of them signaled the gift of the Third Person of the Holy Trinity: the bond of love between the Father and the Son, which has animated the Church ever since that first Pentecost. Recently Pope Francis offered the Holy Sacrifice of the Mass in that upper room, invoking the Holy Spirit upon the bread and wine so that they might become the Body and Blood of Christ. That conjunction of things heavenly and earthly happens every day at Mass. The Holy Spirit thus saves the Church from being a museum of memories and gives it life from age to age, "ever ancient, ever new." All the language surrounding Pentecost is about newness: "Kindle in them the fire of Thy love . . . and Thou shalt renew the face of the earth."

In confirmation the Holy Spirit blesses the soul with gifts of wisdom, understanding, counsel, fortitude, knowledge, piety, and fear of the Lord.

The seven gifts enliven the intellect and the will, just as the Spirit of God breathed upon creation in seven stages. In speaking of character from the position of a detached philosopher, Aristotle emphasized three qualities of a well-integrated personality: *ethos* (an honest use of talent); *logos* (an honest use of the mind); and *pathos* (an honest involvement with the sufferings of the world). The Holy Spirit shifts this into a supernatural dimension by an ethos that lets God guide human talent, a logos that perceives the ultimate truth of God behind all lesser truths, and a pathos that unites human suffering with the suffering of Christ, turning tragedy into triumph.

The Holy Spirit thus unites all human expression into one joyful song, as John Donne wrote:

> Bring us, O Lord God, at our last awakening into the house and gate of heaven, to enter into that gate and dwell in that house, where there shall be no darkness nor dazzling, but one equal light; no noise nor silence, but one equal music; no fears nor hopes, but one equal possession; no ends nor beginnings, but one equal eternity, in the habitations of thy glory and dominion, world without end. Amen.

June 8, 2014

The Gift of the Endless "Now"

All that Our Lord had planned by His Incarnation, death, Resurrection, and Ascension is fulfilled when He fills the Church with the Holy Spirit. Life cannot be seen, and it is known only by being lived. Thus, the life of the Church, lived through our own lives, makes Pentecost an ageless presence. We do not look back on the day when the Holy Spirit was given, for that day is an "endless now." The Church enables us to enter eternity in time, most immediately in the Holy Eucharist, for eternity is not so much "timelessness"—which term we use in time to define what is beyond time—as it is awareness of God. "Now this is eternal life, that they should know you, the only true God, and the one whom you sent, Jesus Christ" (John 17:3).

Last Sunday the largest number of children in the history of our parish made their First Communion with Our Lord. They are very young, but in that moment they became two thousand years old, and, more accurately, they entered heaven on earth. Today, one of our liveliest parishioners, Margaret Bradshaw, celebrates her 106th birthday, with vivid memories of her First Communion nearly a century ago, as one of the first beneficiaries of the decision of Pope St. Pius X to extend Communion to children. She gets younger with each Communion.

All this is the measureless gift that Christ gives us by letting us share in the bond of love between Him and His Father. "Pour out Your Spirit" we pray on Pentecost, but only because the Holy Spirit has already moved us to want Him. A fourth-century inscription on the gravestone of a Christian in Asia Minor expresses the hope of all who have received the

Holy Spirit: "Here sleeps the blessed Chione, who has found Jerusalem, for she prayed much."

Pope Benedict XVI is the ninth Pope in the lifetime of Margaret Bradshaw. Remembering his own First Communion in 1936, the Pope recently told a child: "I understood that Jesus had entered my heart, He had actually visited me. And with Jesus, God Himself was with me. And I realized that this is a gift of love that is truly worth more than all the other things that life can give."

June 12, 2011

The Blessed Trinity

Sanctus! Sanctus! Sanctus!

While there are natural evidences for the existence of God, only God Himself can reveal to us the mystery of the Holy Trinity. St. Paul says that we can cry out, "Abba, Father" only because of the Holy Spirit, who "bears witness with our spirit that we are children of God" (Rom. 8:15–16), and none of us can say that Christ is the Second Person of the Holy Trinity unless the Holy Spirit has taught us (1 Cor. 12:3).

This is why the feast of the Holy Trinity is celebrated on the Sunday after Pentecost, when the Holy Spirit taught the Apostles the mystery of the Three-in-One and One-in-Three. Had we invented God, He would not be a complex mystery beyond our unaided intelligence. In recent years, for culturally conditioned motives, some have tried to reject the divine inspiration by replacing the Trinitarian names with "Creator, Redeemer, and Sanctifier," which is a "Modalist" heresy, for it implies that the Three Persons are different roles that God slips into for performing different functions. All Three Persons create and redeem and make us holy.

Since the Holy Trinity is the source and center of the Gospel, the Church did not think it necessary to have a special feast to celebrate this fact for about a thousand years. Special veneration of the mystery spread in France, and Thomas Becket brought it to England in the twelfth century. Pope John XXII, one of the Avignon Popes living in France, made it a universal feast in 1334, and in 1911 Pope St. Pius X made it a solemnity, which is the highest kind of feast. This is to be remembered when people think that the liturgical calendar is fixed and unchangeable.

A creed named for St. Athanasius, who was exiled five times in the fifth century for his defense of the divine nature of Christ, is a prime object of meditation on this day. It is included in this week's bulletin and should remind us that the highest gift we have from Heaven is God's revelation of His inner being to us mere mortals. Every misunderstanding about God, in one way or another, comes from denying what the Holy Spirit has taught the Church. To think of God only as Creator is a rather passive kind of inert deism, and to think of Him only as the Incarnate Son easily becomes humanism, and to focus only on the Holy Spirit becomes an emotional kind of spiritualism.

In tribute to the heavenly mystery, we have the privilege of invoking the Father and the Son and the Holy Spirit as we make the Sign of the Cross, for Christ Crucified gives us access to the glory of His Father and the Spirit: "No one knows who the Son is except the Father, or who the Father is except the Son and anyone to whom the Son chooses to reveal him" (Luke 10:22).

May 18, 2008

Truth or Blasphemy

The Constitution of Ireland begins: "In the name of the Most Holy Trinity, from Whom is all authority and to Whom, as our final end, all actions both of men and States must be referred, / We, the people of Éire, / Humbly acknowledging all our obligations to our Divine Lord, Jesus Christ . . ."

The landslide vote in Eire for legalizing the fictitious form of marriage between persons of the same sex, in contradiction of all laws natural and divine, unearths the pulsating Druidism that St. Patrick and his fellow saints defied. The estimated $17 million from pressure groups in the United States is no excuse, for people will be pressured only if they are willing to be pressured. Another dismal fact is that more than 90 percent of the young people influenced to subscribe to this vote were formed in Catholic schools. The vote was less in favor of inversion and more in hostility to a Church whose Jansenism and clericalism had incubated corruption and lassitude. While most of Europe suffers from the deadly sin of indifference, or sloth, Ireland is in adolescent rebellion, virulent and irrational. This was exploited by political interests hostile to Christian civilization, and their propaganda combined legitimate accusations against ecclesial failings with a left-wing, secularist agenda.

Ireland helped to bring the Faith to America, and when the flourishing of that Faith degenerated here, that donation was returned in the form of a bacillus. Ireland today has among the highest rates of suicide and mental illness in all Europe, and one-third of children there are born out of wedlock. Things are worse in the United States. Look at the St. Patrick's Day Parade in New York City to see what happens when the honor of a saint is dishonored, and when ambassadors for Christ become nothing more than goodwill ambassadors.

What happened in Ireland was not sudden. Like a dead elephant that remains standing for a short while before collapsing, so the Flame that Patrick kindled on Tara had died long before Catholicism was mixed up with political causes, and ethnic drollery replaced dogma. In mordant irony, just a few weeks ago, the Stormont in Northern Ireland rejected a motion favoring same-sex unions, a motion more indicting for having been introduced by the Sinn Féin, which had long persuaded naïve Americans that it was a Catholic cause.

The archbishop of Dublin, hardly a firebrand, said: "Marriage is not simply about a wedding ceremony or about two people being in love with each other. Marriage, in the Constitution, is linked with the family and with a concept of family and the mutuality of man and woman as the foundation for the family."

In light of the fine invocation of the Irish Constitution, the Irish vote is worse than perverse: it is blasphemous. All the great saints of once-verdant Ireland would have used stronger language.

May 31, 2015

Teaching Us Everything

The feast of the Holy Trinity is an exclamation punctuating the joyous days following Christ's Resurrection. Throughout His earthly ministry, the Second Person of the Trinity kept hinting at this deepest of all mysteries, as when He said that those who saw Him saw the Father, and that the Father and He are one, and again when He breathed the Holy Spirit on the apostles so that they might forgive sins. It was only as He ascended in glory that He explicitly announced the Father and the Son and the Holy Spirit.

It is a paradox of our age's pedantic arrogance that it tends to think of earlier cultures as rough and clumsy, while affecting exasperation at the subtlety of their language. As the Church prepares to use, later this year, a more precise translation of the Creed, there are those who say that the terminology will confuse ordinary people. The Fathers of the Council of Nicaea (AD 325), and later Constantinople (AD 381), did not think that their formulas were only for philosophers. Some were gifted thinkers. But it is said that Bishop Nicholas of Myra (known by many today as Santa Claus) was so unsubtle that he punched the heretic Arius in lieu of debate.

We understand easily only what we have made. When it comes to what someone else has invented (for me, the computer is an annoying example), it is harder. When it comes to the Second Person of the Holy Trinity—who was not created at all—it is impossible to understand Him without His help. So Jesus sent the Holy Spirit to "teach you everything" (John 14:26).

The new English translation of the Creed will speak precisely as the Holy Spirit did when He led the early bishops to speak in their own

Greek, using words such as "only begotten" and "consubstantial." The subapostolic Fathers were free of the bias infecting second-rate intellectuals, who suppose that deep thoughts are too obscure for anyone other than their extraordinary selves. St. Paul was an evangelical failure once when he tried to be a rhetorical success, endeavoring to persuade the professors in the Areopagus university by quoting their own authorities. He certainly had done his research, but he might have been more successful had he quoted Jesus of Nazareth instead of Epimenides of Knossos and Aratus of Soli.

Yesterday was not atypical in our parish. Within about eight hours, I offered the Sacrifice of the Mass twice, heard confessions, baptized a baby, married a young couple, and buried a man. Each of these actions was done in the name of the Father and the Son and the Holy Spirit, in whom "we live and move and have our being" (Acts 17:28). Though some of the Greek poets had used similar words, the Word of God made them real. That is why St. Paul died in Rome, not for a syllogist, but for a Savior.

June 19, 2011

Radiance, Power, and Grace

St. Elizabeth of the Trinity was a French Carmelite who died in 1906, having lived only twenty-six years, but the greatest theologians would attest that she was their peer in apprehending the deepest mystery of the Faith. St. Thomas Aquinas said that his mystical encounter with the heart of Heaven was so wonderful that everything he had ever written was "so much straw," which is saying a lot, since his works are among the greatest thoughts ever recorded. So it is more appropriate to say that the Trinity is apprehended rather than comprehended, for God is beyond all human intelligence. But Jesus explains it: "I have called you friends, for everything that I learned from my Father I have made known to you" (John 15:15). So it is no surprise that even young Elizabeth of the Trinity was able to approach this mystery.

Saint Athanasius wrote:

> Even the gifts that the Spirit dispenses to individuals are given by the Father through the Word. For all that belongs to the Father belongs also to the Son, and so the graces given by the Son in the Spirit are true gifts of the Father. Similarly, when the Spirit dwells in us, the Word who bestows the Spirit is in us too, and the Father is present in the Word. This is the meaning of the text: My Father and I will come to him and make our home with him. For where the light is, there also is the radiance; and where the radiance is, there too are its power and its resplendent grace.

Having revealed the fact of the Holy Trinity, God left it to humans to find language capable of expressing it. So the *Catechism* explains: "In order to articulate the dogma of the Trinity, the Church had to develop her own terminology with the help of certain notions of philosophical origin: 'substance,' 'person' or 'hypostasis,' 'relation,' and so on. In doing this, she did not submit the faith to human wisdom, but gave a new and unprecedented meaning to these terms, which from then on would be used to signify an ineffable mystery, 'infinitely beyond all that we can humanly understand.'"[5]

If that seems complicated, there is the prayer of the young Elizabeth of the Trinity:

> O my God, Trinity whom I adore, help me forget myself entirely so to establish myself in You, unmovable and peaceful as if my soul were already in eternity. May nothing be able to trouble my peace or make me leave You, O my unchanging God, but may each minute bring me more deeply into Your mystery! Grant my soul peace. Make it Your heaven, Your beloved dwelling, and the place of Your rest. May I never abandon You there, but may I be there, whole and entire, completely vigilant in my faith, entirely adoring, and wholly given over to Your creative action.

May 22, 2016

[5] CCC 251, quoting Paul VI, *Credo of the People of God*, no. 2.

THE MYSTERY OF FATHERHOOD

On May 29, when the secretary of Housing and Urban Development, Mel Martinez, was in the parish, I spoke at a dinner given for him and remarked that it was the 550th anniversary of the fall of Constantinople to the Turks, the 189th anniversary of the death of Josephine Bonaparte, and the 264th birthday of Patrick Henry. We call these coincidences. But coincidences are sometimes ways that divine providence shows the mysteries of God at work. It is providential that this year the feast of the Holy Trinity is celebrated on our nation's official Father's Day. Civil holidays like that come and go at the will of the government, and the Holy Trinity preexists all government and the universe itself, but fathers are not incidental, nor is the doctrine of the Fatherhood of God.

The dignity of fatherhood is known by knowing God. There are those who would suggest the Fatherhood of God is a psychological self-projection of a patriarchal society. This nonsense is an old heresy known as Gnosticism. The opposite is true. The social order fully knows the meaning of fatherhood only as an emanation of the Fatherhood of God. Christianity is virtually unique in its understanding of this. Even the Jews, chosen of God, usually referred to God as Father only symbolically, or metaphorically. The overwhelming science of the Fatherhood of God comes to us through Christ. As we know of the Holy Trinity by revelation, the feast of the Holy Trinity is celebrated on the Sunday following Pentecost, when the Holy Spirit, the Third Person of the Holy Trinity, led the Church into all truth.

Adoration of the Holy Trinity sanctifies and unites earthly families. Neglect of the Holy Trinity leads to family breakdown, sexual confusion, and social chaos. In many parts of our country, the majority of children have been abandoned by fathers. Young men often are fearful of taking on the dignity and duty of fatherhood. The catastrophic depopulation of Europe, which now is beyond demographic repair in the next several generations, is a bewildering consequence of this, and one rarely acknowledged because of social timidity to do anything about it.

As a priest is a father of his parish family, he is deeply moved by the young fathers in the parish who are Christs in their homes, loving their wives as Christ loves His Church and caring for their children as Christ laid down His life for His sheep. This is a glorious mystery, flowing from the power of the Father and the Son and the Holy Spirit. The *Catechism* teaches: "The mystery of the Most Holy Trinity is the central mystery of Christian faith and life. It is the mystery of God in himself. It is therefore the source of all the other mysteries of faith, the light that enlightens them" (no. 234).

June 15, 2003

Prayer, Suffering, and Miracles

On June 16, Padre Pio (1887–1968) will be canonized as St. Pio of Pietrelcina. One of the largest crowds ever to gather in Rome will attend the solemn rites, for he was one of the Church's most astonishing miracle workers. The miracles are indications of his sanctity, but his holiness consisted of something even more impressive.

In 1971, Pope Paul VI said: "Look what fame he has had, what world clientele has gathered around him! But why? Was it because he was a philosopher? Was it because he was wise? Was it because he was a man of means? It was because he said the Mass humbly, he heard confessions from morning to night, and he was, difficult to say, a stamped representative of the stigmata of Our Lord. He was a man of prayer and suffering."

As a priest and consecrated religious, St. Pio was "Padre." Civilization has been built by good fathers, and the Liturgy invokes "Abraham our Father in Faith" and all the patriarchs as witnesses. Washington is the father of our country, and Lincoln was Father Abraham to an afflicted people. Father's Day is a civil tribute to the fatherhood that begins with God our Father, from whom all earthly fathers take their name. Bad fathers betray their families and their civilization. That is true of fathers of children and of our spiritual fathers who are bishops and priests. The Church is suffering today because many fathers have failed to obey the model of our Holy Father, the Pope.

These months will see the canonization of some great men, each a model of some expression of fatherhood. I want to have a little temporary shrine to Padre Pio in the church, and to do this for some of the others too. Our Church and our culture need a good sweeping out by good fathers who will lead their children in the ways of righteousness. The way to keep a right focus in these days is to focus on the saints. The media have a way of ignoring the miracles of the saints, because they are inexplicable unless you admit the truth of Catholicism.

Fatherhood is a masterwork of virtue. The decree of Padre Pio's beatification in 1997 said: "It is certain that the Servant of God, Pio of Pietrelcina, to the world Francesco Forgione, professed Priest of the Order of Friars Minor Capuchin, has practiced to an heroic degree the theological virtues of faith, hope and charity, both towards God and towards neighbor, as well as the cardinal virtues of prudence, justice, fortitude, temperance, and the attached virtues."

It is sad for the moment that there are problems in the Church caused by irreverence and immorality. It is wonderful that the Church's other problem is that we are getting more saints than we can find room for on the calendar and our altars.

June 16, 2002

Words of Truth and Reason

Having spent more than a few years dealing with mental patients, I thought I was pretty well informed about the etiology of psychosis. But one day I had to deal with an especially distressed individual whose symptoms were unlike any I had encountered. I asked a distinguished psychiatrist if there were a diagnosis for such a personality. He replied that, based on the information I had given him, the best term was "nutcase."

That was precisely what the Roman governor Porcius Festus thought of St. Paul. The apostle had been imprisoned by the previous governor, Felix, for causing social unrest. The problem was that Paul's alleged crimes had to do with religion, and the cynical Romans did not want to get involved in matters concerning Judaism or indeed anything outside the Roman legal system. As the Greeks were by nature philosophers, so the Romans were above all lawyers. When the King of Galilee, Julius Marcus Agrippa II, visited Festus in the coastal city of Caesarea with his sister, Julian Berenice of Cilicia (with whom he was said to have had an incestuous relationship), Festus described to them with Roman disdain this Paul of Tarsus, who spoke of "a certain Jesus who had died, but who Paul claimed was alive" (Acts 25:19).

After Paul testified before King Agrippa, Festus shouted, "You are mad, Paul; such language is driving you mad!" He assumed Paul was an ivory-tower Hebrew intellectual—unlike sturdy Romans, who built real towers and aqueducts and bridges. But Paul said, "I am not mad, most excellent Festus. I am speaking words of truth and reason." Agrippa remarked, only half in jest, "You will soon persuade me to play the Christian" (Acts 26:24–28).

Christians here are engaged in a confrontation with our national authorities that resembles St. Paul's trials.[6] As in Rome, some in authority assume that anyone who believes in a "certain Jesus who had died but who Paul claimed was alive" must be mad. With admirable unity, the Catholic bishops are defying our present government. This discomfits vague Catholics who prefer Caesar and his largesse to Christ and His sacrifice.

I recently received a note saying that our bishops are exaggerating the state of things to mislead the people. I should be glad to disprove that in public debate—for there is no substance to such a view—but the note was anonymous. Paul was not mad, and we celebrate the mystery that will always be a puzzle to those who define reality on their own terms: "The grace of the Lord Jesus Christ and the love of God and the fellowship of the Holy Spirit be with all of you" (2 Cor. 13:13).

June 3, 2012

[6] While promoting his federal takeover of medical care, the 2010 Affordable Care Act (ACA), then-President Obama promised that nothing in the measure would violate First Amendment religious freedoms. Yet by 2011, Mr. Obama and his administration were demanding that *all* employers pay for employee medical policies that cover acts that plainly violate Catholic teaching, such as contraception, sterilization, and abortion—including, ludicrously, such employers as the Little Sisters of the Poor, a religious community founded in 1839 to care for the elderly poor. Mr. Obama and his attorney general insisted that the Sisters comply under threat of fines. The Little Sisters sued in federal court. Legal challenges to the ACA continue in the courts as of this writing—half a half past the end of the Obama presidency.

The ACA may be dismantled piecemeal. In 2014 in *Burwell v. Hobby Lobby*, the U.S. Supreme Court declared that the act violates the First Amendment rights of closely held businesses. In 2016, the Court rebuffed Obama's defense against the Little Sisters' suit by remanding it to the lower courts. In 2017, President Trump, who had supported the Little Sisters during campaign debates, issued an executive order protecting the Sisters and promised that their legal ordeal would "soon be over."

The Body and Blood of Christ

Corpus Christi

The greatest gift of God to us is Himself in the Holy Eucharist. Pentecost Sunday celebrated the coming of the Holy Spirit into the Church, and Trinity Sunday celebrated the central mystery of the Faith, the dogma of the Holy Trinity. Today, in a feast formally decreed by Pope Urban IV in 1264, the celebration of the Body of Christ, Corpus Christi, becomes a celebration of a celebration, for it rejoices in the Eucharistic action during which the Church prays to God the Father, invoking God the Holy Spirit to change the bread and wine into the Body and Blood of God the Son. All this is a unified action, indeed a sacred dance, ritualizing the unity and harmony of the Three Persons of the Holy Trinity.

In the Eucharist, the priest prays: *Ut hoc sacrificium meum ac vestrum acceptabile fiat apud Deum Patrem omnipotentem* (that this sacrifice—mine and yours—may be acceptable to God the almighty Father). This can be confusing in the current English translation of the Mass, which renders it as "our sacrifice." The listener might not pick up that the priest and the faithful are making different sacrifices. The priest offers the sacrifice of Christ Himself. To this, the people add the sacrifice of their own selves: their souls, their bodies, and their possessions. That is why money and other gifts are offered, as signs of the week's work.

The host and the wine are then discerned by the agency of the same Holy Spirit as Christ's true Body and Blood. Then, the inspired faithful are able to pray to God as "Our Father who art in heaven." The title "God" is now replaced by the intimate identity He has revealed. "Because you are his sons, God sent the Spirit of his Son into our hearts, the Spirit who calls out, '*Abba*, Father'" (Gal. 4:6; cf. Rom. 8:15). As Pope Francis recently said, "The Eucharist is like the 'burning bush' in which the Trinity humbly dwells and communicates itself: this is why the Church has placed the feast of the Body of the Lord after that of the Trinity."[7] So the Eucharist encounters the inner mystery of the I AM as the Triune God.

The Church is a tabernacle for the altar of the Eucharist, and each of us becomes a tabernacle for our Eucharistic Lord when we receive Him in Communion.

I was at the deathbed of a friend who had spent time in a Nazi prisoner-of-war camp. For the rest of his life—nearly seventy years—he thanked the Holy Trinity by regularly attending Nocturnal Devotion. While only mortal, kneeling before the Blessed Sacrament, he had the inestimable privilege that all of us have, of singing with all the angels and saints: *Kadosh, Kadosh, Kadosh. Sanctus, Sanctus, Sanctus*. Holy, Holy, Holy.

June 22, 2014

[7] Kerri Lenartowick, "Pope Invites Romans, Pilgrims to Eucharistic Procession," Catholic News Agency, June 15, 2014.

A Return to the Presence

Last week all of us were happily moved by the first Communions of some of the children of the parish. Aesthetically and ascetically, in beauty and in truth, I think all of us prayed that we might be able to make our Communion with Our Lord as directly and purely as did our newest communicants. He is truly with us, Body and Blood, Soul and Divinity, in a mystery beyond all adequate description but which the saints of the Church have called transubstantiation and have fallen down and adored.

This is the heart of Christian life. Some ardent Christians who seek the power of the Holy Spirit have grown impatient with the forms of worship that Jesus Himself ordained and have drifted off into various heretical sects. Others continue to call themselves Catholics while substituting their own minds for the Infinite Wisdom that comes to us under the outward appearances of bread and wine. It is sad to seek Christ and settle for a substitute, but this is what the sectarians do when they remove themselves from the Real Presence of Christ in the Eucharist.

I recently received a letter from a couple in California who came to the fullness of Faith by reading the Fathers of the Church on the mystery of the Eucharist. By God's grace they survived a superficial catechesis in preparation for their reception into the Church. On a subsequent visit to Manhattan, they came into our church and saw Our Lord enshrined in the tabernacle and were guided in making a good confession. A national Catholic newspaper also recently featured our tabernacle in a front-page article, remarking how the restoration of the Real Presence in the center of the sanctuary has issued in many conversions. "I, if I be lifted up, will draw all men unto myself" (John 12:32). No longer is the pastor's chair high and lifted up. Christ is.

Poor catechesis has obscured this. A result has been that the majority of people who call themselves Catholics (a majority!) in the United States no longer discern Our Lord as truly present in the Mass. The Holy Spirit has begun a powerful return to the truth. Pope Benedict XVI is praying powerfully for this, and we should offer our confessions and Communions to strengthen his hope. The archbishop of Denver, Charles Chaput, recently said: "Whenever the Church is criticized, she understands herself better and is purified. And when she's purified, then she better serves the Lord. We're at a time for the Church in our country when some Catholics—too many—are discovering that they've gradually become non-Catholics who happen to go to Mass. That's sad and difficult and a judgment on a generation of Catholic leadership. But it may be exactly the moment of truth the Church needs."[8]

May 29, 2005

[8] Archbishop Charles J. Chaput, O.F.M. Cap., "It's a Matter of Honesty: To Receive Communion, We Need to Be in Communion," *Denver Catholic Register*, May 26, 2004.

Pouring Light from Her Hands

Heretics usually start out with a sincere desire to make obscure things clearer. A case in point is trying to explain the Real Presence of Christ in the sacred species of the altar by concentrating on Him alone. Some speak rather cloyingly of "going to say hello to Jesus," as if a Holy Hour were a courtesy call on a retired clergyman. And there are, sad to say, some priests who have a compulsive twitch to change the words of the Mass when they raise the Host, so that instead of "Behold the Lamb of God," they will say, "This is Jesus." The problem with these expressions is not that they are wrong, for they are right—but they are not right enough.

The Holy Eucharist brings the undivided God to us, and Christ makes visible the divine indivisibility. What the Three Persons are in themselves is what They are to each other, and what They do is not done in the isolation of One from the Others. When the Host is lifted at the altar, the Holy Spirit recalls to the hearts of the faithful the words of Jesus: "He who has seen me has seen the Father" (John 14:9).

Today a bishop, as a successor of the apostles, will give a number of our children their first Communion and will confirm some with the sevenfold gifts of the Holy Spirit. It is hoped that when they are older, the Holy Spirit will have made them more able to explain the Eucharist. But they will never be more open to God's grace than in this time of innocence. The three little children in Fatima encountered the Eucharist more profoundly than any doctor of divinity. In 1916, the year before Our Lady appeared to them, they saw the "Angel of Portugal" suspended in the air and prostrate before a Host from which drops of blood poured into a chalice. The angel then gave the children Communion: "Take and drink the Body and Blood of Jesus Christ." On May 13, 1917, the mother of God appeared to the children with light pouring onto them from her hands. By a common inspiration, the untutored children knelt and repeated: "O most Holy Trinity, I adore You! My God, my God, I love You in the most Blessed Sacrament!" The daughter of the Father and mother of the Son and spouse of the Holy Spirit was joining them in Eucharistic praise of the Most Holy Trinity.

June 6, 2010

Flesh and Truth

Devotees of Gilbert and Sullivan's *Iolanthe* know the lament of Strephon, who was half man and half woodland sprite: "My body can creep through a keyhole, but what's the good of that when my legs are left kicking behind?" This came to mind when a picture of Bruce Jenner dressed as a woman appeared on a magazine cover. He received ESPN's Arthur Ashe Courage Award for having "shown the courage to embrace a truth that had been hidden for years." Sixty-five years, that is.

Anyone listening to the conversations of sedentary former athletes on ESPN is perhaps not seeking the deeper significance of things, but the declaration that a man is a woman must astonish alert minds—including the Olympic judges who awarded Mr. Jenner a medal under the impression that he was a man.

The longest-simmering heresy in Christian history is Gnosticism, which opposes things spiritual to things material, with the consequence that one's authentic identity is "trapped" in the body. The Christian knows that the body is a temple and not a prison. Philosophers like Immanuel Kant gave Gnosticism a sophisticated veneer, but the invariable result is a creature like Strephon—in mind one thing and in body something else.

John Milton wrote, "The mind is its own place, and in itself can make a heaven of hell, a hell of heaven." Modernity paid the price for opting in favor of Gnosticism when the myth of Superman replacing God led to a world war. In 1941, Cardinal Gerlier preached in Lyons: "The world of the future will be Christian or it will be hell."

Our culture is succumbing to a predilection for a mental construct that seems not far from hellish. I received a questionnaire from Google asking me to check: (1) male (2) female, or (3) other. The book of Revelation (22:15) speaks of *pharmakos*—with reference to illusions induced by drugs. Real science prefers truth to *pharmakos*, even when the truth at first may seem only a hypothesis. In 1965, the Johns Hopkins Hospital pioneered "sex-change" surgery. Since "gender" is a grammatical term with no proper application to biology, the term "transgenderism" had not yet been coined. Such surgery has been stopped there, and Dr. Paul R. McHugh, Distinguished Service Professor of Psychiatry at the Johns Hopkins University School of Medicine, explains that changing one's sex is "biologically impossible," that those who want to do so are mentally ill, and that those who promote what is now called "sex-reassignment surgery" are encouraging mental disorder. Women make excellent women, but men do not. The imitation is bound to caricature feminine grace, as if the ideal woman were Mae West on steroids.

Pope Francis compared the destructiveness of gender confusion and its consequent mutilation to the effects of nuclear annihilation, adding: "Let's think also of genetic manipulation, of the manipulation of life, or of the gender theory, that does not recognize the order of creation."

June 14, 2015

“Never Did Man Speak Like This Man”

The seasonal allergy of commencement addresses with their platitudes and grandiosities is now ending, and most of them will be wiped from memory by the healing unction of time. I read one particularly ineloquent speech that cannot easily be forgotten because of the nonchalant way the speaker unleashed a cataract of tasteless humor and crude language. He even mocked the words of the school's motto, which is a quotation of the Word of God.

The evaporation of erudition in our universities has made celebrity more important than science, to the point where degree ceremonies are addressed by entertainers instead of scholars. There is no equilibrium in this: the number of lame comedians speaking at graduations is greater than the number of philologists speaking at the Oscar ceremonies. More foreboding is the way the confusion of fame with integrity is applauded by reasonably intelligent people. The coarsening of speech turns from thesis to fact when it degrades even those who have had some vestigial acquaintance with high culture.

Two thousand years ago, a voice cried out in the wilderness announcing the approach of the Word of God in the flesh. Then the Word spoke: “Amen, amen I say to you, unless you eat the flesh of the Son of Man and drink his blood, you do not have life within you” (John 6:53). In response, “many of his disciples returned to their former way of life, and no longer accompanied Him. Jesus then said to the Twelve, ‘Do you also want to leave?’ Simon Peter answered him, ‘Master, to whom shall we go? You have the words of eternal life’ “ (John 6:66–68).

In the succession of Simon Peter, Benedict XVI led the faithful on the feast of Corpus Christi, bidding a fractious culture not to return to its former way of life. With degraded voices all around—the shrill echoes of proud people who once thought their academies and economies would last forever—Christ speaks to us by His true presence in the Eucharist, Body and Blood, Soul and Divinity. His priest at the altar invokes the same power that made the universe out of nothing.

Christ the Living Word condescends to come among us so that we might not be vulgarized, and He allows Himself to be mocked, so that we are not demeaned. That is why, after hearing Jesus, even skeptics said what no one has ever been able to say at the end of a graduation speech, however worthy or ignoble: "Never has a man spoken the way this man speaks" (John 7:46).

June 26, 2011

Desire and Illusion

A young city boy on his first camping trip woke his father at dawn and said, as he gazed out of his tent, "Look, Dad, the sun is rising just like on TV." Our present generation, of which we are privileged to be a laggard part, does not find it easy to distinguish actuality from artifice. In the background is a reluctance to acknowledge that an impression of reality is not the same as reality itself. This is symptomatic of what Pope Benedict XVI called the "dictatorship of relativism."

By that he meant the notion absorbed by people bereft of logic, that what one wants something to be, comes to be—simply by the wanting. This has immediate and desultory influence on moral conduct. Like the little boy who thought that the real sun looked like the cartoon sun on television (or, like the nice woman who told me that the altar flowers were so lovely that she thought they were artificial), people may reject the concrete facts of nature and posture that their desires are legitimate just because they are desired. A lurid example of this is the redefinition of marriage to make that organic and divine institution nothing more than a fantasy of one's arrested emotional development, the product of a plebiscite, and the opinion of judges in solemn robes. Polls and parliaments are willing tyrants when the mob consents to be tyrannized by their opinions and decrees.

G. K. Chesterton gently slapped his readers back to reality from egoistic comas when he wrote in his *Short History of England*: "To have the right to do a thing is not at all the same as to be right in doing it." So when someone says, "I am free to do what I want with my body," you may be impelled by charity and justice to reply that he is indeed so free, but if he defies the law of gravity, the pavement quickly will be of a different opinion, and if he says there is no difference between a man and a woman, two shades named Adam and Eve will rise up with mocking smiles.

Those who have long sipped the intoxicating nectar of false perception may hesitate to draw a line between desire and dogma, fabrication and fact. If reality is nothing more than the visible costume of an impression, impressive tyrants will orchestrate that fantasy from their balconies, with rhetoric to mold malleable minds. The long legacy of demagoguery attests that weak points persuade people if the points are shouted loudly enough to overwhelm reason. Opinion polls shout, and network "talking heads" shout, and Internet pundits shout, but then there is a "still, small voice" that does not fade away: the long and logical echo of "*Fiat Lux*" uttered by the real Creator of the real universe.

June 7, 2015

Civilization — the Gift of Martyrs

The film *Cabaret* is better known these days than the novel *The Berlin Stories*, on which its screenplay is based. Christopher Isherwood described the dissolute culture of a demoralized people that gave rise to the National Socialists. Heroes in the German Church defied the Nazi outrages, and thousands became martyrs. Bishops who honored the apostolic witness included Michael von Faulhauber, Bl. August von Galen, Konrad von Preysing, and Josef Frings, while some others were satisfied to adjust to those barbaric times. The heroes had not much support from the papal nuncio to Germany at the time, Cesare Orsenigo, who told Preysing: "Charity is well and good, but the greatest charity is not to make problems for the Church." The German bishops made a better showing than the Tudor bishops, who all caved in to Henry VIII—save John Fisher, who became the only saint among them.

Pope Benedict XVI, who lived during the hard days in Germany, said in 2002: "Heroic virtue properly speaking does not mean that one has done great things by oneself, but rather that in one's life there appear realities which the person has not done himself, because he has been transparent and ready for the work of God."[9] This is the universal call to holiness about which St. Francis de Sales preached so solidly.

Recently, the German cardinal Walter Kasper has described a "Revolution of Tenderness and Love" that would seem paler than the bold summons of Pope Benedict and St. Francis de Sales. In 2014, Cardinal

[9] Cardinal Joseph Ratzinger, "Letting God Work" (article published on the occasion of Josemaría Escrivá's canonization, June 10, 2002).

Kasper said: "Heroism is not for the average Christian."[10] Many seem to have accepted that, for the German Church is in demographic meltdown: priestly ordinations have dropped by half in the last decade, and Mass attendance has plummeted to 10.4 percent. This contrasts with the amazing growth of the Church in Africa—but Cardinal Kasper has said: "They should not tell us too much what we have to do."[11]

Last Sunday, a parade down Fifth Avenue with its raucous obscenities surpassed in decadence anything described in *The Berlin Stories*. At the same time, I was accompanying a group of visiting "wounded warriors" from Walter Reed Hospital unable to get through the traffic. One young soldier strove to carry his luggage with two prosthetic arms, while trying not to look at the street vulgarity. Such heroism is precisely what bewilders those who take pride only in their lack of heroism. Hilaire Belloc wrote:

> The Barbarian hopes—and that is the very mark of him—that he can have his cake and eat it too. He will consume what civilisation has slowly produced after generations of selection and effort, but he will not be at pains to replace such goods, nor indeed has he a comprehension of the virtue that has brought them into being. Discipline seems to him irrational, on which account he is ever marveling that civilisation should have offended him with priests and soldiers.

July 2, 2017

[10] "Cardinal Kasper: 'Heroism Is Not for the Average Christian,'" Catholic News Agency, May 9, 2014, http://www.catholicnewsagency.com/.

[11] "Kasper's Comments Breed Online Controversy over Racism Charges," Catholic News Agency, October 17, 2014.

The Shoulders of Giants

There is a curious study in an academic journal of psychology. The study—titled *Intelligence*—claims that we in the twenty-first century have an average IQ fourteen points lower than the Victorians', a calculation based on how long the brain takes to react. The scientist author claims that this is the result of a backward form of natural selection, with the most intelligent people tending to have fewer children (usually for the wrong reasons), while others now tend to live longer. Some of this smacks of the false science of eugenics, but it is a counterargument to what has been called chronological arrogance, which assumes that people today are smarter than those of the past.

This arrogance is a form of perpetual adolescence, as it thinks the elders of the past were not very bright. But the very existence of civilizations attests to the fact that we have inherited what we did not invent. In 1676, Isaac Newton wrote: "If I have seen a little further, it is by standing on the shoulders of Giants." This is the common sense that is common only to uncommon minds. The theologian John of Salisbury said the same thing in 1159: "We are like dwarfs sitting on the shoulders of giants. We see more, and things that are more distant, than they did, not because our sight is superior or because we are taller than they, but because they raise us up, and by their great stature add to ours."

The gigantic theological minds gave us the doctrine of the Holy Eucharist, and less subtle minds in our time find it hard to accept because they will not stand on the shoulders of those theological minds. Or, nearly as bad, thinkers of modest stature may end up shrinking the magnificent Scholastic teaching on Eucharistic transubstantiation into a cloying caricature, with images of a baby Jesus curled up in the Tabernacle. The great Eucharistic Doctors never separated the Body and Blood of Christ from the mystery of the Holy Trinity. St. Catherine of Siena never thought of measuring IQs. She is a Doctor of the Church, even though she was practically illiterate. We should pray as she did:

> O Trinity! Eternal Trinity! O Fire, abyss of Love!
> Would it not have been enough to create us after
> your own image and likeness,
> causing us to be reborn through grace and by the Blood
> of Your Son?
> Was it still necessary that You should give us even the
> Holy Trinity as food for our souls?
> Yes, Your love willed this, O Eternal Trinity.
> You gave us not only Your Word through Redemption
> and in the Eucharist.
> But You also gave us Yourself in Your fullness of Love
> for Your creature.
> Truly the soul possesses You, Who are the supreme
> Goodness.

June 2, 2013

Plumbing the Depths of Death

The dramatic events surrounding the death of Pope John Paul II and the election of Pope Benedict XVI could have obscured the observances of the Holy Year of the Eucharist except for the fact that everything done as a Christian is Eucharistic. Funerals and inaugurals are centered on the Holy Sacrifice of the Mass. Pope Benedict's first trip was last Sunday to a Eucharistic Congress in Bari, where he celebrated the Sacred Liturgy before 180,000 people and renewed an appeal for reunion with the Eastern churches. The Holy Father is now escorted on his travels outside the Vatican by the Swiss Guards who formerly attended him only in the Vatican. Their elegant armor belies the fact that they are modern soldiers, armed with modern weaponry. The new Pope has also enlisted a more conspicuous presence of deacons to attend him at the altar in ancient custom.

The only way to make a worthy Communion is to make a humble confession. In our parish, I am edified by the increase of confessions. It means more saints. We now have more confessions than in easier days when there were more priests here. Sometimes I have to stop hearing confessions to offer a second Mass. Most people understand this. A few say that this is inconvenient for them. This is a distress to me, but unless they have borne sons who now are priests, they have no right to complain. Only saints can bilocate.

Do meditate on these words of Pope Benedict XVI:

> The Eucharist is far more than just a meal; it has cost a death to provide it, and the majesty of death is present in it. Whenever

we hold it, we should be filled with reverence in the face of this mystery, with awe in the surface of this mysterious death that has become a present reality in our midst. Certainly the overcoming of this death in the Resurrection is present at the same time, and we can therefore celebrate this death as the feast of life, as the transformation of the world. In all ages, and among all peoples, the ultimate aim of men in their festivals has been to open the door of death. For as long as it does not touch on this question, a festival remains superficial, mere entertainment to anaesthetize oneself. Death is the ultimate question, and wherever it is bracketed out there can be no real answer. Only when this question is answered can men truly celebrate and be free. The Christian feast, the Eucharist, plumbs the very depths of death. It is not just a matter of pious discourse and entertainment, of some kind of religious beautification, spreading a pious gloss on the world; it plumbs the very depths of existence, which it calls death, and strikes out an upward path to life, the life that overcomes death.[12]

June 5, 2005

[12] Joseph Cardinal Ratzinger, "The Wellspring of Life from the Side of the Lord, Opened in Loving Sacrifice," in *God Is Near Us: The Eucharist, the Heart of Life* (San Francisco: Ignatius Press, 2012).

Why Did God Love the World?

Our Lord's admonition that much will be required of those to whom much has been given applies most vividly to us. We have been given so much in the way of inventions and medicine and comparative wealth, but above all, in knowledge of the world around us. No king in his silken bed at Versailles knew the luxury of instant information that we have. YouTube gives us access to great music for which the Bourbon monarchs had to summon their court musicians, while we need only press a button on the computer.

I have been listening on YouTube to the choir of St. Paul's Cathedral in London singing the Victorian John Stainer's setting of John 3:16: "For God so loved the world that he gave his only begotten Son so that everyone who believes in him might not perish but have everlasting life." They are the most wondrous and mysterious words ever spoken and have to be sung, for they are a love song. A young man shyly told me that he knelt to propose marriage to the girl he loved, even though he thought she might laugh at him. But in the humility of true love, he meant what he said, and they are now married.

God so loved the world. That means all He has created in the world. I confess that I do not yet share my Creator's affection for all things. For instance, I do not like, let alone love, mosquitoes. Perhaps Our Lord sees, through His aesthetic lens, a mathematical symmetry and power of endurance that I will appreciate only during my first years of assimilation in Purgatory. For that matter, I find it hard to like, let alone love, some of the people rambling along Thirty-Fourth Street at a snail's pace, oblivious to those behind them, and speaking loudly and rudely on their cell phones. I am not God, who loves them as I try only feebly to do. He even died for them. And for me.

Jesus became human, but from the perspective of heavenly glory, He might just as easily have become a mosquito. In the divine eye, humans are no more or less attractive than bugs, but God took upon Himself the form of a slave (Phil. 2:7) because humans have the unique gift of reciprocating the love that made them. By reflecting that love, through worship and service, we are God's agents in making the world into what He wants it to be.

I am not a mosquito, but that makes no difference to my Creator. In the seventeenth-century words of Samuel Crossman, now accessible on YouTube:

My song is love unknown,
My Saviour's love to me;
Love to the loveless shown,
That they might lovely be.
O who am I,
That for my sake
My Lord should take
Frail flesh and die?

June 18, 2017

The Faith Entrusted to Us

In these days of transition in the political life of our nation and in cultures East and West, such as we see in the intense growth of Christianity in former communist lands while the Faith is increasingly suppressed in formerly Christian countries, including our own, we are going through a social earthquake not unlike the transition of the Roman republic into an imperium. Our own nation increasingly indulges luxury and selfishness while rejecting its foundational principles, just as decadent Romans from the second century onward could hardly connect with the virtuous ideals of the former republic. The Founding Fathers of our country would be bewildered by the ignorance, vulgarity, and opulence that permeate politics today.

That said, the opportunities to work for Christ as His stewards are unparalleled, given the fertile minds and astonishing means of communication available to the Church today. It is the nature of a bureaucracy, even in the Church, to promote mediocrity and to perpetuate corruption, but true Christians have unsurpassed means to defy and deny that calcification of the gospel.

The noble pagan Cicero knew how to be clever with politics and was not pristine in practicing what he preached, but he never forgot the best of his culture and even went into exile for opposing what was unworthy of Rome. Bereft of any mystical intuition beyond the cultic superstition of his day, which his innate cynicism tempered, he revealed the best in himself when he called natural gratitude the "parent" of all the other virtues. He was speaking of life in the earthly city of Rome, which some still call the Eternal City. He was unaware of the true Eternal

City spoken of by Christ, nor did he know of an ultimate and superior gratitude, which is the Holy Eucharist.

For ourselves, we know of that Eucharist and must live a life of constant gratitude for it, lest we take it for granted. In daily commerce, we must also be grateful to God for giving us life and, for those in this parish, for being able to live that life in this neighborhood, which is undergoing the fastest and most exhilarating development in the history of our country. As "Hell's Kitchen" becomes the spectacularly energized and wealthy "Hudson Yards," we should always remember it for what it was and be grateful to God for making us actors in the social drama currently playing here. Our souls would be endangered were we to luxuriate in the commercial and residential construction around us. This demographic gift is an assignment from God: "From everyone to whom much has been given, much will be required; and from him to whom much has been entrusted, even more will be asked" (Luke 12:48). God will show us what to do and how to do it if we give Him thanks for the chance and the challenge.

June 5, 2016

Peace, and What It Truly Means

Our Savior gives us peace "not as the world gives" (John 14:27). Worldly peace is an absence of violence. Christ's peace is Himself. When He rose from the dead, He said "Peace" as an announcement of His presence. This peace is not an absence of violence, for it involves a violent confrontation with the Prince of Lies, who denies that Christ is the Prince of Peace. Thus, pacifism is contrary to Christianity, for it is a naïve denial of the power of evil.

After the Our Father, Christ as the Lamb of Sacrifice being present on the altar, the priest asks Christ to grant us the peace and unity of His Kingdom. In the traditional Roman Rite, he kisses the altar, which has become the Throne of the Lamb, and offers the people the peace of Christ. It is optional for the priest to bid the people greet each other with a sign of peace. This sign of peace has become for many a high point of the Mass, for they mistakenly think that it is a rite of socialization during which we greet each other in a friendly way. The exchange of peace is properly a formal greeting by which the faithful announce to each other that the Risen Christ is giving us the peace of Heaven. The priest is forbidden by the rubrics to leave the sanctuary and exchange this, for his greeting is the voice of Christ, to which the people react in announcing that the Lamb of Sacrifice is about to give them in Holy Communion, "the peace which passes all understanding" (Phil. 4:7). This is passed from bishop to priest to deacon to the faithful in a hierarchical structure representing the organic harmony of the Church.

As bad money drives out the good, so is there the tendency for banal culture to "dumb down" our sense of worship. The ritual embrace of peace has usually become a handshake and a "Hello there, how are you?" Poor instruction has led people to think that this is just a fraternal greeting, and that the Mass is not complete without it. This surprises some because we need better to learn the meaning of the sacred mysteries that the Pope is trying to teach us through his new encyclical on the Eucharist. I am always edified by the reverence of our people, in stark contrast often to visitors who come to weddings here with no sense of the sacred space or how to behave in the House of God. One wonders what their concept of worship is. *Lex orandi lex credendi*—the way we pray indicates what we believe.

June 1, 2003

Eternal Witness

Among the joys of parish life is witnessing marriages, and while many people do not realize how much planning is involved to meet the canonical norms for the sacrament of holy matrimony, the day of marriage always is radiant, whatever the weather outside may be. Our most recent wedding, on June 7, was that of Eduardo Abreu and Kristen Novack. It was the 320th in this parish since I have been pastor, but each one of them seems like the first.

Every couple is different, and each enriches the parish with their family stories, to which their marriage will add new chapters. Our newest groom, Eduardo, is the great-great-nephew of the late Archbishop of Caracas, Monsignor Castillo Hernández, and great-nephew of His Eminence Rosalio José Cardinal Castillo Lara, who died last year at the age of eighty-five and who confirmed Eduardo in the Vatican. Cardinal Castillo Lara's life is a reminder of the powerful witness Christians are called to make in our day against oppression. The cardinal was a leader of the cause of democracy and the Church's rights against a government grown increasingly hostile to Catholicism.

He was born in Venezuela's Aragua State. The third of seven children, he was ordained a priest in the Salesian Order in 1949. The next year, he began canon law studies in Turin and later became a professor of law in Turin and Rome before returning to Venezuela, where he eventually became titular archbishop of Precausa. In 1985 Pope John Paul II created him a cardinal, and he returned to Rome, where he served as president of the Administration of the Patrimony of the Holy See and the Pontifical Commission for the State of Vatican City.

As a spiritual shepherd, the cardinal's attentions were never far from his homeland, and he provided outspoken support for his countrymen as their new government evidenced more and more Marxist tendencies. The Venezuelan president, Hugo Chávez, is not known for understatement and on the day the Archbishop of Caracas, Ignacio Cardinal Velasco, died in 2003, Mr. Chávez cursed Cardinal Velasco and threw stones, and then held up a picture of the archbishop wearing devil horns. The elderly Cardinal Castillo Lara was brave to return in retirement, fully aware that the Venezuelan president had called him "a hypocrite, bandit, and devil with a cassock." The cardinal's anxious concern for his fellow Venezuelans sickened him, and he died of cardiac arrest on the day the government changed the national constitution.

Unlike Cuba, the current government of Venezuela has vast oil reserves and other sources of wealth to finance its agenda, but one trusts that the Catholic bishops and faithful people will use their spiritual resources in a contest that history has seen repeated many times.[13] The future promise is in clear voices of shepherds like Cardinal Castillo Lara and the buoyant hope of young people consecrating themselves to God in Holy Orders, the religious life, and Holy Matrimony.

June 8, 2008

[13] Nine years have passed since this was written. Venezuela's wealth is gone, but its war against its people and the Catholic Faith continues, for the present. As a result of the Marxist policies of Chávez and his successor, Nicolás Maduro—gutting the constitution and replacing it with price controls, inflation, a state takeover of industries, and slave labor—Venezuela is predictably bankrupt, its people are starving, and there are near-daily street protests, with scores of deaths as the state attempts to suppress them.

Saints for Our Time

Last week the Church celebrated the feast of the Martyrs of Uganda. In the late nineteenth century, French and English missionaries were welcomed by King Mutesa I of Buganda in the southern part of modern Uganda. His successor, Mwanga II, however, was a youth who became a persecutor of Christians and all foreigners. He especially opposed Christian morality, as it contradicted his affinity for unnatural vice—which was abhorred by the local Buganda culture, but which he is said to have learned from Arab tradesmen. The young male pages of Mwanga's court were Christian converts and refused the king's attempts at seduction. This disobedience to the king was considered treasonous, and Mwanga exercised what he considered his right to destroy any life at will, according to the saying, *Namunswa alya kunswaze*—meaning "the queen ant feeds on her subjects."

Mwanga soon decreed the execution of converts Yusufu Rugarama, Makko Kakumba and Nuwa Sserwanga on January 31, 1885. A senior adviser to the king, Joseph Mukasa Balikuddembe, was beheaded on November 15, 1885, and there were many martyrdoms in the following year, climaxing on June 3, 1886, at Namugongo, with the torture and burning alive of twenty-six, including their leader, Charles Lwanga, a recent convert himself and majordomo of the royal household. Pope Paul VI canonized them in 1964. An icon of St. Charles Lwanga is in our sanctuary.

When Pope Paul went to Uganda as the first Pope to make an apostolic journey to sub-Saharan Africa, he said, "The infamous crime by which these young men were put to death was so unspeakable and so expressive of the times. It shows us clearly that a new people needs a moral foundation, needs new spiritual customs firmly planted—to be handed down to posterity. Symbolically, this crime also reveals that a simple and rough way of life—enriched by many fine human qualities, yet enslaved by its own weakness and corruption—must give way to a more civilized life wherein the higher expressions of the mind and better social conditions prevail."[14]

Alas, the infamous crime of which the Holy Father spoke is now paraded as a civil right in our decaying culture, and some states are making it quasi-sacramental. Our current president promotes it, along with his defense of infanticide, which even King Mwanga II would have found degrading. Pope Francis recently said that one cannot be a Christian if one is not willing to be a martyr. In New York today, Catholics may not face beheading or burning, but their political incorrectness could subject them to the subtle ignominy of social scorn and discrimination. Ours has become a neo-pagan culture, and that can be even worse than a simple pagan culture. Pagans did not know about Christ. Neo-pagans do know about Him and reject Him, so their only defense is the malice of a cynic.

June 9, 2013

[14] Pope Paul VI, homily at the canonization of the Martyrs of Uganda.

"You Have Not Chosen Me, but I Have Chosen You"

In an age of short attention spans, celebrities fade quickly. Rare is the personality who becomes, in the term wrongly and tiresomely used by writers with limited vocabularies, "iconic." An ephemeral perception of things makes it hard to understand public significance apart from celebrity-based "popularity" and "approval ratings."

I mention this because of the continuing celebrations of the Diamond Jubilee of Queen Elizabeth II. It is the nature of her office, and confounding to anyone who does not understand the institution, that she did nothing to earn her position other than being born. But that notion is reassuring to all of us who are made heirs of salvation by the gratuitous mercy of Christ the King.

The distinguished Catholic peer Lord Alton of Liverpool has calculated that during Elizabeth's reign, there have been six popes, and her Catholic subjects have increased from 4.4 to 6.6 million in Britain, and from 25 million to 140 million throughout the Commonwealth. One-third of the primary schools in England are Catholic, and they comprise two-thirds of the most highly rated ones. During the queen's reign, the number of Catholic charities in the United Kingdom has grown to 1,000. In the Commonwealth countries, the Catholic Church runs 5,246 hospitals, 17,530 dispensaries, 577 leprosy clinics, and 15,208 homes for the elderly.

After long centuries of conflicts between state and Church, this is a remarkable record, but it should not distract from the growing threats to religion from secularists throughout the world, and increasingly so in our own nation. Through it all, Elizabeth II has displayed a constant sense of duty and responsibility, knowing that with the perquisites of her office comes an unrelenting publicity that will not cease until her last breath—far different from public figures who may hope to retire and play golf. The example of growing old gracefully and publicly is another gift of a monarch—in contrast to mere celebrities who use the limelight to create an illusion of agelessness. It is said that when a Hollywood starlet, about to be presented to the queen, worried that the colors of their dresses might clash, she was told that Her Majesty does not notice what others are wearing.

The longest-reigning Pope was St. Peter, who may have been Bishop of Rome from AD 29 to 67. Blessed Pope Pius IX reigned nearly thirty-two years. A monarch, but more than a monarch, and a "servant of the servants" as Vicar of Christ, who came not to be served but to serve, each Pope knows that however long or short his years may be, or however popular or unpopular he may be, his authority is not conferred by human applause, but by the One who said, "You have not chosen me, but I have chosen you, that you should go and bear fruit, and that your fruit should remain" (John 15:16).

June 10, 2012

Denial

At a vigil service before the burial of a friend who was a Knight of Malta, a comfortable attorney who was a self-styled progressivist took umbrage at a phrase I had read from the daily prayer of that order: "Be it mine to practice and defend the Catholic, the Apostolic, the Roman faith against the enemies of religion." He told me that there are no enemies of religion anymore. When Our Lord sent His disciples out, He told them what to expect, and disabused them of such dangerous naïveté. They would be lambs among wolves, and not lambs among lambs.

In little more than a dozen years, the Christian population in Iraq has dropped from 2 million to 300,000.[15] In Syria, where Christians once were 10 percent of the population, there are fewer than a million now,[16] and many of them are being kidnapped and held for ransom at $100,000 each. The misery of enslavement, destruction of churches, crucifixions, and beheadings was brought into sharp focus last March, when sixteen people were gunned down in a nursing home, including four Indian religious sisters of Blessed Teresa's Missionaries of Charity who were caring for them. That may have been the efficient cause for the U.S. State Department to declare, after long tarrying, that all this is deliberate genocide.

In *Lord Jim*, Joseph Conrad wrote, "No man ever understands quite his own artful dodges to escape from the grim shadow of self-knowledge."

[15] The Christian population in Iraq is estimated to have slipped to 250,000 in the year since this column was written.

[16] The latest estimates put Syrians Christians at fewer than 500,000.

Artful denial is a common disposition among those who do not want to compromise their ideology with reality, lest they be discomfited by confrontation with evil.

The Turkish government persists in denying the genocide of 1.5 million Armenians between 1915 and 1923. Japan still denies the massacre of hundreds of thousands of Chinese in 1937 during the Second Sino-Japanese War. Not until 1994 did Russia accept full responsibility for the slaughter of 21,857 Polish officers, clergy, and academics in the Katyn forest. At the time, President Franklin Roosevelt blamed that massacre on the Nazis and exiled to American Samoa the navy officer George Earle, who had produced the facts.

In that same year of 1943, Roosevelt received in the Oval Office the Catholic layman Jan Karski, who had heroically microfilmed evidence of the German concentration camps, but the president wanted only to talk about farm horses. Even Supreme Court Justice Felix Frankfurter later wrote: "I did not say that [Karski] was lying. I said that I could not believe him. There is a difference." George Orwell called the obliteration of conscience in the face of malice "doublethink." The psychological term is "dissociation."

Our parish is blessed to have as its patron St. Michael the Archangel, and his "defense against the wickedness and snares of the Devil" is not the last resort but the first in our perpetual spiritual combat. That is why on Sundays we invoke him at the end of Mass.

June 12, 2016

"Mr. Gorbachev, Tear Down This Wall"

Our Pope has called President Reagan "a noble soul." Addressing the parliament of Portugal, Reagan became the first president to mention Our Lady of Fatima. He recalled how the Pope went to Fatima after the attempt on his life, "to fulfill his special devotion to Mary." He added, "In the prayers of simple people everywhere, simple people like the children of Fatima, there resides more power than in all the great armies and statesmen of the world." When Communist members of the parliament stormed out, the president drew laughter: "I notice that those on the Left have found their seats uncomfortable."

Many of our own cultural elite were uncomfortable when, on March 8, 1983, Reagan called the Soviet Union an "Evil Empire." Anthony Lewis of the *New York Times* said the speech was "primitive ... simplistic theology," and Henry Steele Commager of Columbia University called it "the worst speech ever given by an American president." But when news of the speech reached Natan Sharansky, confined to an eight-by-ten-foot cell on the Siberian border, the reaction was different: "Tapping on walls and talking through toilets, word of Reagan's 'provocation' quickly spread throughout the prison. We dissidents were ecstatic. Finally, the leader of the free world had spoken the truth—a truth that burned inside the heart of each and every one of us."

I catechized and received into the Church a friend, Peter Robinson, who went on as presidential speechwriter in 1987 to pen the line, "Mr. Gorbachev, tear down this wall." Various advisers demanded it be removed, but President Reagan shouted it in Berlin, and soon the wall came down.

In the 1970s, when I did not know who he was, the man walked across a meeting room in a Philadelphia hotel where I was to speak. "Hello, Father, my name is Ronald Reagan." Soon, everyone knew who he was, but some patronized him as just a "great communicator." He said, "I am not a great communicator, but I communicate great things." Mother Teresa visited him in June after he was shot and told him, "You have suffered the passion of the cross and have received grace. There is a purpose to this.... This has happened to you at this time because your country and the world need you."

On January 14, 1988, he signed a document: "Now therefore I, Ronald Reagan, President of the United States of America, by virtue of the authority vested in me by the Constitution and laws of the United States, do hereby proclaim and declare the unalienable personhood of every American, from the moment of conception until natural death, and I do proclaim, ordain, and declare that I will take care that the Constitution and laws of the United States are faithfully executed for the protection of America's unborn children."

Only those who support that are fit for public office.

June 13, 2004

The Heart of a Hero

These last few days saw thousands of priests from around the world gathered in Rome to honor Pope Benedict XVI as "Servant of the Servants of God," concluding the celebration of the Year for Priests. The Pope knows that the priesthood is the sign of Christ's sacrifice, and therefore it always will be a contradiction of false values. And, as a contradiction, it will especially be an offense during those phases of civilization that reject a higher vision of human purpose. Priests themselves have to be reminded of this daily.

The concept of sacrifice, alien to a culture of self-assertion, is the foundation of moral strength. Friedrich Nietzsche, the philosopher of power, mocked Christ's willing submission to suffering for others and thought that the beatitude delivered on the Mount—"Blessed are the meek"—constituted a "slave mentality." He did not realize that "meek," as used here, is rooted in the Greek word *paos* and means the kind of discipline that tames a wild animal and makes it able to put its strength to useful purpose, which is why the meek, so disciplined, inherit the earth. The priest must be tamed by the Holy Spirit so that his holy meekness will also strengthen the faithful. Nietzsche went insane, and it is said that his breaking point was when he watched a horse being beaten by its owner and could not reconcile this cruelty with his theories of "man as superman." St. John Vianney was the meekest, and strongest, of men and said that a true understanding of the priesthood would not drive us insane; rather it would make us die—"not out of fear, but out of love."

In a show of heroic meekness, 30 Catholic priests were killed last year on various continents, the highest number in the last 10 years. Last

Sunday in Warsaw, more than 140,000 people attended the beatification of Father Jerzy Popieluzsko, who was beaten to death by Communist agents and tossed into a reservoir in 1984 at the age of 37. Since then, 17 million pilgrims have visited his tomb. His mother led the faithful in praying before his relics at the beatification. Saints are stronger than supermen.

Last month, Pope Benedict XVI spoke of the priesthood when he went to Fatima and was heard by a throng even larger than the crowds that welcomed Pope John Paul II in 2000. He told half a million people, "We must cultivate an interior watchfulness of the heart which, for most of the time, we do not possess on account of the powerful pressure exerted by outside realities and the images and concerns which fill our soul."[17]

This is the power of holy meekness, which inherits the earth. The end of the Year for Priests is the beginning of a renewed response to St. John Vianney's definition: "The priesthood is the love of the heart of Jesus."

June 13, 2010

[17] Pope Benedict XVI, homily at the beatification of Francisco and Jacinta Marto, Fatima, May 13, 2010.

Corinth, New York

The last Sunday of June will end the Holy Year of St. Paul, commemorating the two thousandth anniversary of his birth. The end, of course, should be the beginning of a new reverence for his teachings. In the liturgies of these weeks, there is an emphasis on his two letters to the Corinthians. They have never been more timely.

Corinth was a Greek city located south of Athens in the area connecting the Peloponnesus to the mainland. In the arts and sciences, it excelled and it produced some engineering marvels. It was full of energy, much of it uncontrolled, and money was the real god, although everything sensual was extolled. The temple of Aphrodite at one point housed one thousand cultic prostitutes, and every sort of fantastic superstition was tolerated. In very many ways, it was like New York City. Just as we say, "If you can make it in New York, you can make it anywhere," the Romans who took over the city said, "Not for everyone is the journey to Corinth."

St. Paul was a brave man to preach the gospel there, and it is no surprise that he had severe difficulties. Unlike the Galatians, whose caution about doing the wrong thing bordered on scrupulosity, the Corinthians were tempted to think "anything goes." Their lush cosmopolitan environment, symbolized by the third architectural order—which was the most elaborate, in contrast to the Doric and Ionic—tolerated any kind of behavior and philosophy, so long as it was aesthetically satisfying. They were heavily influenced by the Gnostic notion that the spiritual world has nothing to do with the material world. They compartmentalized their existence, thinking that they could engage in high, abstract thoughts while living dissolute lives. A sacramental sense of creation was alien to the Corinthians, like some New Yorkers who prefer to speak of "spirituality" rather than Christianity, who think they can be Catholic without confession, and "do what they want with their own bodies" while ignoring the sacredness of life, fornicating and cohabiting outside the marriage bond, and sanctioning perversions as "alternative lifestyles."

After St. Paul established the Church in Corinth in about AD 51, he wrote to them from Ephesus in Turkey, reminding them, sometimes with tears, that the human body is a temple of the Holy Spirit. He knew how hard it was for the Corinthians to be countercultural, as a Christian must be in a pagan environment. He was never discouraged, nor did he "lower the bar" by watering down doctrine like a false evangelist hoping to attract crowds by preaching a nonthreatening, generic gospel. Instead, he blesses the raucous Corinthian flock with a highly developed, Trinitarian theology: "May the grace of the Lord Jesus Christ, and the love of God, and the fellowship of the Holy Spirit be with you all" (2 Cor. 13:13).

June 14, 2009

Obedience — and Thanksgiving

Writing a weekly message to you is a challenge even under ordinary circumstances, because the cruel regimen of the printer requires that it be done in 480 words or fewer. Usually I spin it off on a Monday morning, which is not the most inspiring time in the week for most people. In the twelve years that I have been pastor of the Church of Our Saviour, I have written many hundreds of columns, and of them all, none has been more daunting for me than this one. In 480 words I must explain that I shall be moving on to a new position, albeit for the same Savior who has been so patient with me as a poor priest of his since Cardinal Cooke ordained me in the Lady Chapel of St. Patrick's Cathedral on September 8, 1981. I promised obedience to the cardinal and to his successors, and I have done that and continue to do that and shall do that until all my earthly shepherds turn me over to the Chief Shepherd, who I hope will spare the rod and comfort me more with His staff.

I was gratified that so many wanted me to stay here, and Cardinal Dolan was not unaware of that when he decided that he has other tasks for me to undertake. The Church is vaster than any particular parish, beloved as ours is for many far and wide, and while I am moving to the far other end of our island on the West Side, it is not like going to the moon. I am to be pastor of St. Michael's Church near Pennsylvania Station and administrator of Holy Innocents Church in the Garment District. St. Michael's is on the southern perimeter of what New Yorkers long ago came to call "Hell's Kitchen," but that is not the Hell from whose fires we pray to be saved. It is actually a quickly changing neighborhood, and I shall have some responsibility for extending the work of the Church to meet the needs of the residences and new businesses that are expanding there.

I have until August 1 to say in various ways what I cannot say in a few lines of print. Cardinal Egan officially appointed me your pastor in the tumultuous week following the attacks on September 11, 2001. Our city has undergone unimaginable changes since then, and I think it may be said that our parish has also changed greatly. I am thankful for all the blessings we have received here and for all those who have been a blessing to me. These twelve years have been a lifetime counted one way, but counted another way they have been "short as the watch that ends the night." Instead of squeezing all my thoughts into 480 words, I shall uncharacteristically refrain from words and let my prayers thank God for all He has done.

June 16, 2013

Coercion

The bishops of the United States have called for daily prayer leading up to the Fourth of July to safeguard freedom of religion in our country. That freedom is tenuous these days. There seems to be a conscious attempt by the federal government, in speech after speech, to replace freedom of religion with freedom of worship. That is not as subtle as it seems, for while permitting ritual acts of devotion within the walls of a building, it would limit the right to express one's religious beliefs in public discourse. This applies to everything from displaying religious symbols to preaching and publishing outside the confines of a house of worship. In Orwellian semantics, soon enough, even the commandment to love the sinner but hate the sin becomes "hate speech."

There are some religions, like some governments, that are intrinsically hostile to freedom of religion. Recently, a Christian in Tunisia was martyred for converting from Islam, and his killers chanted prayers against "polytheists," as they call Christians, while slowly slicing off his head. This happens frequently, yet our own government and much of the media are conspicuously silent. While they may not be interested in religious creeds, they seem tacitly to oppose what the Second Vatican Council's Declaration on Religious Freedom urged, which is to grant citizens who wish to practice their faith "immunity from coercion in civil society." Perhaps there are those highly placed in our culture who would prefer to retain the option of religious—or antireligious—coercion.

The Council said, "The Truth cannot impose itself except by virtue of its own truth." To guarantee freedom of religion is not to suggest that all religions are the same or equally true. Such indifferentism is deaf to

Christ, who declares that He is the Truth itself. God proposes Himself to us, without imposing Himself. "Choose this day whom you will serve" (Josh. 24:15). But once one makes that free choice, the intrinsic power of Christ goes to work. Thus, He can say, without any compromise of our free will: "It was not you who chose me, but I who chose you" (John 15:16).

In art, Impressionism depicts how an object is perceived. Another school of modern art called Expressionism shuns objects altogether and uses distortion to express the artist's emotional state. Some secularists, even in high places of our culture, think of religious belief as Expressionism—such as Matthew Arnold, who called religion "morality touched with emotion." If one lives that way, the morality disappears, all that remains is emotion, and shouting replaces creeds.

The truth of Christ frees believers from the tyranny of emotion and defies the widespread, imperious attempts to exploit human need by replacing Mother Church with the Nanny State. Cultural Expressionists may genuinely think that belief in God is just wishful thinking. This ignores the fact that Christ chooses us before we choose Him—for instance, when he took St. Paul by surprise. So the apostle, among the first in a long line of martyrs, would say, "I received from the Lord what I also handed on to you" (1 Cor. 11:23).

June 17, 2012

The Full Stature of Christ

St. Anthony, whose feast we recently celebrated, was an Augustinian canon in Portugal who joined the new Franciscan Order in 1220, having been moved by the martyrdom of five Franciscans who had been beheaded by Muslims in Morocco. The year before, during the Fifth Crusade, St. Francis of Assisi narrowly escaped execution when he preached the gospel to Egyptian Muslims who had killed about five thousand Christians a few days before in Damietta. Anthony went to Morocco but became gravely ill, worked his way home via Sicily, and spent the rest of his thirty-six years preaching a combination of loving patience and mercy with bold insistence on Christ's truth and stern reproof of lax clerics.

This is to be remembered when many voices today equate doctrinal orthodoxy with "rigidity" and portray the moral demands of Christ as distant ideals, if not impractical encumbrances. St. Anthony preached against the fanatical Albigensian heretics in southern France, whose misunderstanding of creation denigrated marriage and family life while promoting abortion, sodomy, and assisted suicide. They considered themselves more "spiritual" than Catholic "doctors of the law" and took Pharisaic pride in boasting that they were not Pharisees. Bold St. Anthony was not an "Albigensian-phobe," and reasonable people now are not phobic when they tell the truth about mental illness dressed as "transgenderism," about borders open to illegal immigrants described as hospitality, or about denial of constitutionally guaranteed religious freedom justified by the courts as contributing to some improvised idea of social good.

The first Christians knew well the degrading course of systemic moral corruption (cf. 1 Cor. 6:9–10; 1 Tim. 1:8–11). They would not have been surprised at how the Canadian High Court has condoned forms of bestiality, the government of Massachusetts no longer identifies femaleness and maleness as biological categories, people weep when a gorilla is shot to save the life of a human child, and a student in a major university is given a light slap on the wrist for violating a young woman while being complimented for his athletic ability. But they would have been astonished at the politically correct reluctance to identify the religious motivation of terrorists who massacre people.

In 1951, General Douglas MacArthur said, "History fails to record a single precedent in which nations subject to moral decay have not passed into political and economic decline. There has been either a spiritual awakening to overcome the moral lapse, or a progressive deterioration leading to ultimate national disaster."

A cartoon some years back showed a Lilliputian looking at Gulliver and saying, "Either he's very big or we are very small." In the instance of Christ, it is not either-or. He is very big *and* we are very small. But we need not remain small if by a spiritual awakening we "attain to the unity of faith and knowledge of the Son of God, to mature manhood, to the extent of the full stature of Christ" (Eph. 4:13).

June 19, 2016

The Gift of Prophecy versus Weather Prediction

A museum curator showed me a contemporary copy of the bull *Inter Caetera*, by which Pope Alexander VI divided the world between Spain and Portugal with meridians. While not without effect, it was generally ignored. John Henry Newman's letter to the Duke of Norfolk lists popes who were mistaken in certain policies: St. Victor, Liberius, Gregory XIII, Paul IV, Sixtus V, and St. Peter himself when St. Paul "withstood" him (Gal. 2:11).

Pope Urban XIII and his advisers, in the misunderstood Galileo case, inadequately distinguished the duties of prophecy and politics, and of theological and physical science. John Paul II said, "This led them unduly to transpose into the realm of the doctrine of the faith a question which in fact pertained to scientific investigation." Fr. Stanley Jaki, a physicist, cautioned me against using the "Big Bang" as theological evidence for creation. On a loftier level, the physicist Fr. Georges Lemaître likewise restrained Pope Pius XII from conflating the parallel accounts of the universe.

Fr. Lemaître pioneered the "First Atomic Moment"—contradicting the prevailing thesis of a cosmological constant, or "static infinite" universe. Sir Fred Hoyle mocked it as the "Big Bang," but the term has lost its condescension. Lemaître told the Pope: "As far as I can see, such a theory remains entirely outside any metaphysical or religious question.... It is consonant with Isaiah speaking of the hidden God, hidden even in the beginning of the universe." It was like the counsel of Cardinal Baronius: the Scriptures teach us how to go to heaven, not how the heavens go.

Pope Francis' encyclical on the ecology of the earth is adventurously laden with promise and peril. It can raise consciousness of humans as stewards of creation. To prevent the disdain of more informed scientists generations from now, it must be safeguarded from attempts to exploit it as an endorsement of one scientific theory over another concerning any possible anthropogenic causes of climate change. It is not incumbent upon a Catholic to believe, like Rex Mottram in *Brideshead Revisited*, that a Pope can predict the weather. As a layman in these matters, all I know about climate change is that I have to pay for heating a very big church with an unpredictable apparatus. This is God's house, but He sends me the utility bills.

The first Pope, from his fishing days, had enough hydrometeorology to know that he could not walk on water. Then the Eternal Logos told him to do it, and he did, until he mixed up the sciences of heaven and earth, and began to sink. As vicars of that Logos, popes speak infallibly only on faith and morals. They also have the prophetic duty to correct anyone who, for the propagation of their particular interests, imputes virtual infallibility to papal commentary on physical science while ignoring genuinely infallible teaching on contraception, abortion, marriage, or the mysteries of the Lord of the Universe.

June 21, 2015

Crime and Confession

The outpouring of people in Rome to celebrate the solemn canonization of St. Pio of Pietrelcina on June 16 surpassed all expectations, and the Church is using these days to ask for special favors from his heavenly intercessions. Our temporary shrine to the saint popularly known as Padre Pio is at the St. Jude altar, next to the daily confessional, because St. Pio was as much as anything a confessor of souls.

There has been a goodly increase in daily confessions in our parish, and we have added confession times on Sunday. As our numbers grow, we may also increase the times of Sunday confession. I am grateful to our priests for their help. Recently, the Holy See put to rest a notion that confessions should not overlap with the celebration of the Mass. One must attend the full liturgy to receive Communion, but a recent instruction of the Holy See not only permits but ardently encourages the sacrament of penance to be celebrated in a part of the church as the Sacrifice of the Mass is being offered. Good confessions make good Communions. The Church has suffered in recent years from the sin of presumption, evident in laziness about going to confession.

One of the many blessings attached to the numerous weddings in our parish is the frequent abundance of beautiful flowers decorating the sanctuary. You will agree that they are different from the floral decorations at the funeral of the unrepentant Mr. John Gotti. The press gave the bizarre funeral rites for Mr. Gotti more publicity than the canonization of St. Pio. Crime and the glamour of iniquity fascinate the human imagination because all humans inherit the consequences of the first crime against God, the original sin of wanting to be gods.

Pathetic were the silly people paying gaudy tribute to the gangster, and more pathetic is the fact that many of them received what passes these days for a Catholic education. A reporter for a major New York newspaper wrote that he carried a pink carnation to the wake and touched the coffin as a sign of respect. He could have done better by lighting a candle in front of our image of St. Pio. Evil can hypnotize, but only grace can open our eyes to behold Our Lord face-to-face "and not as a stranger."

June 23, 2002

Christ Crucified

Any young man called to the priesthood must be like St. Paul: "It is no longer I who live, but Christ who lives in me" (Gal. 2:20). This is true of all Christians. *Cupio dissolvi*—"I wish to disappear." Dioceses that understand this excel in vocations, and those that do not, fail.

When I arrived at this parish, there were many liturgical abuses. Let it not be said that these were the predilections of young people, for there were practically none then. Rather, they had become the habit of older people who had simply shifted from perfunctorily expedited Masses and a few sentimental hymns to the fabricated folk Masses of the 1960s. I put a stop to the habit of applauding the organist and the choir. The musicians we have now would be embarrassed by such behavior. Pope Benedict XVI said, "Wherever applause breaks out in the liturgy because of some human achievement, it is a sure sign that the essence of liturgy has totally disappeared and been replaced by a kind of religious entertainment."

There is even a danger of that same narcissism when attempts at a "reform of the reform" become a self-conscious spectacle. Evelyn Waugh said that Anthony Eden was not a gentleman because he dressed too well. We try to offer the best to God, but we must not be fussy about it like the nouveau riche. It once was said that dowagers in Boston did not buy hats, they *had* hats. C. S. Lewis's view was that true worship should be like a good old shoe, so comfortable that you don't have to break it in: "The perfect church service would be one we were almost unaware of; our attention would have been on God." That is a sensibility I have long admired in the Byzantine liturgies. While some speak of the High Mass of the Western Church as the "most beautiful thing this side of Heaven," I know of nothing so formally transcendent and still so informally natural as the Liturgy of St. John Chrysostom.

The constant fidgeting for "theme liturgies" and experimentation is a sign of failure. Worse yet is the priest who solicits laughter like a ham actor in a dying vaudeville show. Such clerics should limit their repertoire to words St. John told the Blessed Mother as her Son bled on the Cross. One is struck by the way Pope Francis, in his personal simplicity and affability, is so enrapt in the solemnity of the Mass that he would not think of smiling through the Sacrifice of Calvary.

It may seem that reform of abuses is as futile as King Canute ordering the tide to roll back. Actually, that great king was showing his court that human pride has no authority over what does not belong to him. That is why he placed his own crown on a figure of Christ Crucified, and that is what true worship is all about.

June 23, 2013

In the Same Arena

This Friday the Church celebrates the martyrdoms of St. Peter and St. Paul in Rome, and the next day, all the early Roman martyrs. Wherever we live, we are united with them in the common Faith entrusted to Peter as Prince of the Apostles and to all in communion with him and his successors, the bishops of Rome, known to us as the popes. On June 3, in Iraq, a thirty-one-year-old priest and three deacons were slain by Muslims at the end of Holy Mass. This young martyr, Father Ragheed Ganni, had studied in my old university in Rome. At his last Mass, he had invoked the ancient Roman martyrs, as is the custom of the Roman Canon, for while there are countless martyrs, the Universal Church names a few of those whose deaths in the city of Peter bind us in common witness to the foundational structure of the Church. As Pope Leo I preached of Rome in the fifth century, "Through the blessed Peter's holy See thou didst attain a wider sway by the worship of God than by earthly government."

The letters of St. Bernard of Clairvaux to his former monk, Pope Eugene III, make clear that nearly a thousand years ago, the city of Rome had its dangers and corruptions, as a thousand years before that, and as today. But Rome is also, as Cardinal Manning wrote, "chosen of God as the center of His kingdom, which is eternal, as the depository of His eternal truths, as the fountain of His graces which lead men to a higher life, as the witness and guardian of law and principles of which the sanction and the fruit are eternal."[18]

[18] Henry Edward Manning, *Miscellanies* (London: Burns and Oates, 1877), 20.

Each feast of the Roman martyrs is an opportunity to affirm our filial bond with the Pope, who now is entrusted with the care of all the churches, as was his first predecessor, the fisherman of Galilee. History bears witness that any attempt to live the Christian life apart from that unity, however sincere and even graceful, will eventually end up in disarray. It may take only a generation, or sometimes several centuries, but ecclesial communities separated from Rome will fragment and fade. This was the message that the young Jesuit, St. Edmund Campion, received from the Pope and saint Charles Borromeo as he prepared to return to his homeland and die a martyr in timeless communion with the Roman saints.

The fourth Pope, Saint Clement I, celebrated the Roman martyrs with words that are also for our present troubled world:

> We are placed in the same arena, and the same contest lies before us. Hence we ought to put aside vain and useless concerns and go straight to the glorious and venerable norm which is our tradition, and we should consider what is good, pleasing and acceptable in the sight of Him who made us.

June 24, 2007

The Spirit of the Music

The maxim that the greatest art is to have no art means that the aim of an accomplishment is to give the impression of effortlessness. An Olympic swimmer does not splash like a man drowning, and a concert pianist glides his fingers over the keys as though it were as natural as breathing. The Italians, who have long experience at it, call this deliberate nonchalance *sprezzatura.*

I have had enough experience of the opera to marvel at how the difficult music is sung as though the singers were blithe canaries. Only from the front seats is the hard breathing and sweating palpable. It is the opposite with bad art and poor artists. Singers of limited talent affect anguish, and this is particularly so with rock entertainers who give the impression of suffering labor pains. The grace with which an artist performs is directly related to the quality of the art. The worse the work, the more pained seems the performer.

Aristotle taught that music imitates the passions or states of the soul, and "when one listens to music that imitates a certain passion, he becomes imbued with the same passion, and if over a long time he habitually listens to music that rouses ignoble passions, his whole character will be shaped to an ignoble form."

Around the year 500, when he was only twenty years old, the Christian philosopher Boethius drew on Aristotle, maintaining that "music is related to us by nature, and ... can ennoble or debase our character."[19] Some of his exquisite writing was set to music a few centuries later and,

[19] Aristotle, *De Institutione Musica,* bk. 1, introduction.

after a score was discovered in a German library, it was performed this year at Cambridge University for the first time in one thousand years. The ethereal experience was a world away from today's popular music.

Knowing that aesthetic barbarians will display their coarseness by severely attacking any critic, it takes courage to say that most modern music is degrading. I trim my courage by hiding behind Plato speaking of certain musicians who corrupted classical culture: "By composing licentious works, and adding to them words as licentious, they have inspired the multitudes with lawlessness and boldness, and made them fancy that they could judge for themselves about melody and song."[20]

When the terrible shootings began in the Parisian theater and the Orlando nightclub, the first reaction was the same: the lamented revelers thought the gunfire was part of the music. They would not have made that mistake had the music been Chopin or Mendelssohn, or the lyre and lute setting for Boethius' *Consolation of Philosophy*. But a decadent culture fatally takes pleasure in pain at high decibels and finds incoherent the logic of God: "I will pray with the spirit, and I will pray with the understanding also: I will sing with the spirit, and I will sing with the understanding also" (1 Cor. 14:15).

June 26, 2016

[20] Plato, *Laws* 3.701.

To Call a Soul to Conversion

This past week the Church celebrated the martyrdoms of St. John Fisher and St. Thomas More. They died in 1535 to defend the papal primacy and the indissolubility of marriage. Thomas More, as a lawyer, knew all the devices of lawyers, which can promote justice or, in craven hands, can thwart it. Amongst all the terrified and compromised bishops of England, Fisher was the only one to defend the truth with his life.

Neither man was impractical in his stratagems, nor did he intemperately invite persecution. They paid the price of honesty rather than await the awful price that a soul eventually pays for compromising the truth. Our nation confronts a graver challenge today. The Church and marriage were the issues then. The issue now is the natural law of life itself.

The archbishop of St. Louis, the Most Reverend Raymond L. Burke, is both a bishop and a lawyer and has a legal competence that charitably shreds emotional equivocation about abortion. In an article in the journal *America* (June 21–28, 2004) he recalls that the bishops of the United States six years ago recognized the difficulties in legislating moral good, but also said that "no appeal to policy, procedure, majority will, or pluralism ever excuses a public official from defending life to the greatest extent possible." A correctly formed conscience cannot be "set in opposition to the moral law or the magisterium of the church" (CCC 2039)." A politician's failure to protect the life of the unborn betrays the public trust.

Canon 915 of the *Code of Canon Law* stipulates that those who "obstinately" persevere "in manifest grave sin are not to be admitted to Holy Communion." This is not a sanction of excommunication arbitrarily imposed by a bishop, as some people describe it. The exclusion is inherent in the nature of the sacrament itself. In other words, culpable individuals have, by their own public defiance of the moral good, excommunicated themselves. A bishop only declares the fact, and that is done when the contempt for the truth has become a public scandal. Unlike other moral matters that may involve prudential interpretation, abortion is a definitive moral evil, and supporting legislation that protects it constitutes formal cooperation in a gravely sinful act. This blatantly obtains in the case of Catholic politicians who support organizations such as Planned Parenthood and the National Abortion Rights Action League.

As in the days of St. John Fisher and St. Thomas More, some fear that opposing "political correctness" might make the situation worse. Reminiscent of Fisher's speech to the legates of England and More's essay on the "Sorrows of Christ"—written in prison—Archbishop Burke writes, "What would be profoundly more sorrowful would be the failure of a bishop to call a soul to conversion, the failure to protect the flock from scandal and the failure to safeguard the worthy reception of Communion."

June 27, 2004

The Savior Who Gave Us Science

On this day of the summer solstice, I think of how much I enjoy the calendar published by the Vatican Observatory, with beautiful photographs of the planets taken with its telescopes at its headquarters on the grounds of the papal summer residence in Castel Gandolfo. Under the direct patronage of the Pope, it is probably the oldest astronomical research institute in the world. Using it, Pope Benedict XVI's predecessor Gregory XIII was able to promulgate the Gregorian calendar in 1582, a tremendous scientific achievement we still use.

In this connection, I am also reminded of a dear friend and great priest who died in Madrid in April, having just given a lecture on science and religion in Rome. Father Stanley Jaki was a member of the Pontifical Academy of Science. He was born in Hungary in 1924 and was trained as a Benedictine monk. Throughout his life, he remained under obedience to the archabbot of Pannonhalma. Eventually he came to the United States and studied physics at Fordham with the Nobel laureate Victor Hess, a pioneer in the study of cosmic rays. Father Jaki lectured throughout the world and was Freemantle Lecturer at Oxford, Hoyt Fellow at Yale, and Gifford Lecturer at Edinburgh. For many years he lived in Princeton and was Distinguished Professor of Physics at Seton Hall. He received the Templeton Prize, the largest monetary award in the world, and used the prize money to help support his brother Benedictine monks. The theme of his more than fifty books was how the Catholic understanding of creation gave rise to modern physics and is the most substantial guide for the right use of theoretical physics and all physical sciences.

I am glad to say that we shared a common affinity for the writings of Newman and Chesterton. While he took no prisoners in academic debates, he had a splendid sense of humor, was an accomplished pianist, and particularly enjoyed the conversations of children. The Rosary was a favorite devotion, and he dutifully kept a daily Holy Hour, which strengthened both his heart and brain. (I don't think he made a distinction between them.)

He often said, "Science lives by hope no less than religion." His own priestly witness gave hope to many in his own day who might otherwise have lapsed into the "ennui" which is the moral infection of our present culture. Indeed, he knew with all great thinkers that there can be no culture without *cult*—which is worship. As Pope Benedict inaugurated the Year for Priests on the feast of the Sacred Heart to help priests live priestly lives, we should also give thanks to the "Savior of Science," as Father Jaki called Our Lord, for priests who have already finished their earthly work.

June 21, 2009

THE SACRED HEART

On Friday, June 19, Pope Benedict XVI inaugurated a special Year for Priests with a special ceremony in St. Peter's Basilica, during which he venerated relics of St. John Marie Vianney, which had been brought from the French village of Ars, where the saint had been parish priest in the nineteenth century. The Pope declared that Vianney, who has been patron saint of *parish* priests, will from now on be patron of *all* priests, whatever their particular priestly work may be.

The Pope chose to begin the Year for Priests, which will include the 150th anniversary of Vianney's death on August 4, on the Solemnity of the Sacred Heart. The Sacred Heart represents Christ's merciful love for the world, as Vianney's own heart, which is one of the preserved relics, represents the saint's love for his parishioners. He once said, "The priesthood is the love for the Heart of Jesus." Pope Benedict XVI echoed those words, saying, "The gift of our priesthood originated directly from that Heart." The Holy Father has said that he wants the year to be a chance for priests to grow in intimacy with the Divine Love and become "in today's world, messengers of hope, reconciliation, and peace."

Not long after I became pastor here, I placed a statue of St. John Vianney, the "Holy Curé d'Ars," in our church. Many were unfamiliar with this saint. Around the same time, I also restored the altar cross and candles, which I found tarnished in the basement. (One individual expressed surprise, being under the impression that Vatican II had abolished this arrangement.) I am gratified now that the Pope has brought Vianney to wider attention, just as he has called for the restoration of altar crosses and lights as we have them here, to emphasize the mystery of the Blessed Sacrament. Since we erected the statue of the Curé d'Ars, our parish has been remarkably blessed with priestly vocations.

The Gospel (Mark 4:38) records a severe storm on the Sea of Galilee during which Our Lord seemed to be asleep in the stern of the boat, His head on a cushion. Pope Benedict has provided this Year for Priests because the world is storm-tossed—politically, economically, morally, and spiritually. Some have thought that God is paying no attention. The fact is that when He seems to be sleeping, He is preparing to calm the storm as Jesus did when He rebuked the wind. Along with that is the other fact, that many Christians have indeed been asleep and now must be awakened. The Pope is calling on priests to do that, but not before they commit themselves anew to the saving power of Christ, who has called them to show people the road to Heaven, as St. John Vianney promised to do when he arrived in that little village of Ars in 1818, and which he did do in an amazing way.

June 28, 2009

All Praise Is His

On September 13, 1224, on the mount of Verna, St. Francis received the stigmata, the marks of Christ's five wounds, in his flesh. Several months later, he composed "The Canticle of the Creatures," now more commonly called "The Canticle of the Sun." It is beautiful in its Umbrian dialect and enchants in any language. The seventh verse, which begins, "*Laudato si, mi Signore, per sora nostra matre terra*," is the incipit of the recent encyclical on the dignity and duties of life in the created order.

Five other verses are quoted in paragraph 87 of the encyclical. They praise the Lord for the sun, moon, stars, wind, air, water, and fire. I am inclined to think that St. Francis, who was a deacon, had in mind the *Benedicite*, which is part of the Liturgy of the Hours, conflating Daniel 3:57–88 and Psalm 148. St. Francis was a walking Bible, and his life was a canticle incarnate, so his inspiration was the same as Daniel's and David's. His canticle distinguishes the creature from the Creator, who is the object of creation's praise.

I found some verses in a Unitarian hymnal:

> Nature shouts from earth and sky,
> In the spring our spirits fly,
> Join the resurrection cry,
> Love is God and fears must die, Alleluia!

Such *poésie* may suit people who are vague about the Resurrection, and it really only works north of the equator. The problem is its inversion of "God is love" and "Love is God." If Love is God, then it is a quick step to thinking of the sun and moon and stars and earth as divine, with earthly pastures as a pantheon.

This is why it is important that "The Canticle of the Sun" be invoked in its entirety. The first and last three verses do not appear in the encyclical. An uninformed reader might get the impression that the saint of Assisi did not sing his song in a transport of joy to God, whose glory is ineffable:

> Most High, all powerful, all good Lord!
> All praise is Yours, all glory, all honor, and all blessing.
> To You alone, Most High, do they belong.
> No mortal lips are worthy to pronounce Your name.

The last three verses praise the Lord for the strength He gives to forgive and to endure sickness and trial, for the mystery of death and fear of dying in mortal sin, and for serving Him *with great humility*.

A satirist once described a trendy clergyman who "collects butterflies and considers the word 'not' to have been interpolated in several of the Commandments." While Christ bid us to "consider the lilies of the field," He did so not as a botanist but as the Lord, who "is before all things, and in him all things hold together" (Matt. 6:28; Col. 1:17).

To redact "The Canticle of the Sun" risks being left with the Sun, but without the Son.

June 28, 2015

With You, Always

There are personal memories, such as those kept in diaries and scrapbooks, and sometimes kept only in the heart. There are collective memories recorded on cenotaphs and invoked on memorial days and shared at family reunions. Cicero said that to be ignorant of the past is to remain always a child. That is not the childlikeness that walks the way to Heaven; it is the childishness that sees no way at all. Moses said, "And you shall remember the whole way that the Lord your God has led you these forty years in the wilderness" (Deut. 8:2). And before that he said, "Then take care lest you forget the Lord, who brought you out of the land of Egypt, out of the house of slavery" (Deut. 6:12).

On the feast of Sts. Peter and Paul, the Church remembers how their deaths planted the Faith in Rome. It is rare for a saint's feast to replace the ordinary propers of the Mass on Sunday. On a wall of the North American College in Rome is inscribed, "*O Roma felix, quae duorum Principum es consecrata glorioso sanguine!*" (O happy Rome, which was consecrated by the glorious blood of the two Princes!)

St. Peter urges us to "remember the words spoken in the past by the holy prophets, and the commandment of the Lord and Savior spoken through your apostles" (2 Pet. 3:2). St. Paul encouraged the Christians in unruly Corinth: "Now I commend you because you remember me in everything and maintain the traditions even as I delivered them to you" (1 Cor. 11:2). These men were very different and did not enjoy compatible temperaments (saints are not inevitably easy to get along with). But they were bound by a holy memory that had changed their lives.

Christianity is what it is because it is much more than that kind of human remembering that when strong is fidelity, and when weak is nostalgia. At the center of Christian living is a kind of hyper-remembering, the Eucharistic *anamnesis*, in both the Roman Canon and the Divine Liturgy of the Easter Church. This is not simply the antidote to amnesia. It is an active participation in what is being remembered. It is the difference between recalling and calling, between representing and presenting. Thus, the Eucharist is the Real Presence of Christ: His Body and Blood, Soul and Divinity.

St. Peter had a vivid memory of the Perfect Victim's Crucifixion, which is why he asked to be crucified upside down, as he felt unworthy to imitate what he remembered seeing on Calvary. And St. Paul could remember every word the Master spoke to him on the Damascus road. They had no need of diaries or scrapbooks, because the Master was with them at the Holy Table, fulfilling His unfailing promise: "I am with you always, even unto the end of the world" (Matt. 28:20).

June 29, 2014

Calling Evil Good

I was with my parents at a performance of Gounod's *Faust* some years ago, and when Marguerite goes mad in act V after killing her baby, my mother let out a gasp that embarrassed me—for we were in a box over stage left, and conspicuous. Now I bless my mother because that maternal empathy is the heart of civilization. "A voice was heard in Ramah, Rachel weeping for her children" (Jer. 31:15). Stifle the mother, and you stifle the child, and the world dies.

Our Lady, being a take-charge kind of woman, as was evident at the wedding in Cana, may have been a midwife often in Nazareth, weeping at the loss of infants—as she surely did when the innocents were massacred in Bethlehem.

In the opera, the repentant Marguerite is taken by angels singing, "Salvation!" But Faust, who bartered his soul to Mephistopheles before fathering Marguerite's child, is bound to that Satan, who, in the words of Milton, bids, "Evil, be thou my good." Anyone who calls evil good moves discourse about infanticide to a very dark place.

On April 26, President Obama, the first sitting president to address Planned Parenthood, not only thanked that organization, which aborts about three hundred thousand children a year, but added, "God bless you." Evil, be thou my good.

On June 13, Nancy Pelosi said that the abortion issue is "sacred ground." Evil, be thou my good.

On June 20, a *New York Times* op-ed contributor described the aborting of her twenty-three-week-old son, who had a heart defect: "I felt my son's budding life end as a doctor inserted a needle through my belly into his tiny heart. As horrible as that moment was—it will live with me forever—I am grateful. We made sure our son was not born only to suffer. He died in a warm and loving place, inside me." Evil, be thou my good.

Our merciful Lord will hear the cry of those who make terrible mistakes, especially those who have not had the grace of being taught right from wrong. To them He offers real angels, and not singers on a stage. But He also predicted, "A time is coming when anyone who kills will think he is offering service to God" (John 16:2). Like Faust, such people ask God to bless destroyers of life, and call the killing fields "sacred ground," and even describe the womb of a mother who kills her child as a "warm and loving place."

Blessed Teresa of Calcutta said that no one is safe around a mother who would kill her own child. Anyone who makes a Faustian bargain knows that even Christ is not safe there: "Inasmuch as you did it to one of the least of these my brethren, you did it to me" (Matt. 25:40). Satan calls evil good.

Christ calls it Crucifixion.

June 30, 2013

Advice and Dissent

Last March 4 the former managing editor of the *New York Times*, Bill Keller, wrote an op-ed essay on scandals in the Church, entitled "Is the Pope Catholic?"[21] It was a diatribe so bitter that many were embarrassed for him. Calling himself a "collapsed Catholic" and not just a "lapsed Catholic," he incoherently attacked doctrine and even stooped to mock the Pope's illness.

On June 29 Keller published another op-ed column recounting his wife's abortion two years earlier. Ultrasound imaging showed a boy, which Keller describes as "a boy-like creature." He resents that "the anti-abortion lobby" gives "tadpole-sized fetuses the poster appeal of full-grown infants." But a father is a father, and Keller remembers "the poetry of the first heartbeats" of the "boy-like creature" he named Charlie.

Tests showed the boy might be born dead or in a "vegetative" state. "Facing the prospect of a greater heartbreak, watching a child die or suffer inconsolably, or exhausting the emotional resources needed for two other children, we decided to end it."

Keller writes that he and his wife had consulted a "nun," who told them, "Think about what God would want, not what the Church would want. They are not always necessarily the same thing." Keller's revulsion at child abusers expressed in earlier columns condemning the Church did not extend to this unhelpful consoler, who thought that *killing* a child might be God's will.

[21] This referred to Pope St. John Paul II, the reigning pontiff.

"The last thing Emma was aware of before surrendering to the anesthetic was Charlie kicking madly."

If this "collapsed Catholic" had obeyed Christ and the Vicar of Christ, whom he considers an "unintelligible" old man "on his last legs"—instead of a dissident nun echoing Eve on the world's first bad day—he would not be disquieted of soul. His wife told him that if there had been no abortion, "we would have lost that baby, but we would not have killed that baby."

That same weekend, the *New York Times* reviewed a book about the Nazi *Einsatzgruppen*, trying to explain the process of "violent socialization" that enabled executioners to sing while babies slowly died on their bayonets. The author's psychological analysis of moral meltdown hauntingly matches the justification of crimes against the unborn in what the Pope has exposed as our "Culture of Death."

Maybe the venomous anger Mr. Keller cast at the Church in his March 4 essay was related to what happened two years ago. Now he senses "a change of heart." Don't call that "Catholic guilt." Guilt is guilt, and the Catholic Church calls it what it is.

A "collapsed Catholic" has collapsed under his own cross. A man so furious at the Church could become a great saint of the Church, like Saul of Tarsus. Mr. Keller has the intelligence and conscience needed. Now he needs humility. He does not need any more advice from a muddled nun who may be less fortunate than he on the Day of Judgment.

July 7, 2002

The Crucible of Liberty

Our parish boundaries cover the twenty-nine acres that were the homestead and farm of the Robert Murray family in the eighteenth century. The Murrays were Irish Quakers who emigrated from County Armagh in 1732. Like many pious people who came to America to do good but who also did well, Mr. Murray became the leading shipping merchant in New York City. His large house, Inclenberg, stood between what are now Thirty-Seventh and Thirty-Sixth streets. On September 15, 1776, his wife, Mary, and her daughters entertained the British general William Howe after his army had arrived at Kip's Bay, a delaying tactic that enabled General George Washington to escape with about four thousand Continental troops.

Mary's son Lindley was thought to have been a Loyalist who fled to England. Actually, he had gone there on business and was forced to stay because of polio. He wrote grammar books that were the most widely used in the United States long after his death in 1826.

For several days in that crucial September of 1776, British and Hessian troops encamped on what is today the site of our church.

As Independence Day draws near, we remember what Ronald Reagan said in his first inaugural address as governor of California in 1967: "Freedom is a fragile thing and is never more than one generation away from extinction." In our generation, the First Amendment right of freedom of religion is threatened in a serious way by mandates of the current executive branch of our government. The bishops of the United States have unanimously called for a Fortnight of Prayer—launched on June 21 in Baltimore, in our nation's oldest cathedral, and culminating on July 4 in the Shrine of the Immaculate Conception in our nation's capital. There, as in all churches, special devotions will be offered for the intentions of Church and state. The bishops have proposed a "Prayer for the Protection of Religious Liberty" for these days:

> O God our Creator,
> Through the power and working of your Holy Spirit,
> You call us to live out our faith in the midst of the world, bringing the light and the saving truth of the Gospel to every corner of society.
> We ask you to bless us in our vigilance for the gift of religious liberty. Give us the strength of mind and heart to readily defend our freedoms when they are threatened; give us courage in making our voices heard on behalf of the rights of your Church and the freedom of conscience of all people of faith.
> Grant, we pray, O heavenly Father, a clear and united voice to all your sons and daughters gathered in your Church in this decisive hour in the history of our nation, so that, with every trial withstood and every danger overcome—for the sake of our children, our grandchildren, and all who come after us—this great land will always be "one nation, under God, indivisible, with liberty and justice for all."
> We ask this through Christ our Lord. Amen.

June 24, 2012

Two Georges

In Independence Hall is preserved a chair crafted in 1779 by the cabinetmaker John Folwell, with a sun on the horizon carved at the top. For nearly three months in 1787, George Washington used it during the Constitutional Convention. Benjamin Franklin mused: "I have . . . often in the course of the session . . . looked at that sun behind the President without being able to tell whether it was rising or setting. But now at length I have the happiness to know it is a rising and not a setting sun." On each subsequent generation falls the obligation to keep that sun rising, a task that requires the virtues that animated Washington, as described by Henry Lee III: "First in war, first in peace, and first in the hearts of his countrymen."

But July 4 is about two Georges, and the sun of King George III is occluded in a mental darkness. Both Georges—true to their name, since it means "husbandman"—loved few things more than farming. Washington let drop his Augustan dignity when he raged at the report that New Yorkers had torn down an equestrian statue of the king in New York City. The horse's tail is preserved in the Museum of the City of New York.

Washington fathered a nation but no children, and perhaps fortunately so, since that precluded the possibility of a dynasty. Names such as Roosevelt, Kennedy, Clinton, and Bush were unknown to him. George III was the loving father of fifteen children and defied court convention by his faithfulness to his queen, Sophia Charlotte. He promoted science, founded Maynooth Seminary for Irish Catholics, and proposed the emancipation of slaves in Virginia, where Jefferson, in contempt for moral consistency, kept slaves while accusing the king of condoning the slave trade.

Great Britain has had its own Declaration of Independence recently in the "Brexit" vote, for good or ill, depending on which pub is polled. But the two Georges shared one assurance as the foundation of all moral liberty—not the rising sun, but the risen Son, whose light never sets: "If the Son therefore shall make you free, ye shall be free indeed" (John 8:36).

July 3, 2016

The Time Predicted by Christ

The Supreme Court's abuse of its authority in the decision redefining marriage as an institution based on feelings rather than fact, and sanctioning deviancy as a civil right, was expected. The surprise was its sentimental substitution of nihilistic narcissism for jurisprudence, expressed in an amorphous substitute for English diction. This passed a death sentence on Christian culture, just as *Roe v. Wade* sanctioned the deaths of millions of infants.

As Christ rose from the dead, so can our nation, but only the cynic and the naïf will deny that the next steps will be attacks on Christ Himself in His Church, schools, and charitable institutions. It can't happen here? That is what the English said before 1534 and the French before 1789 and the Russians before 1917 and the Germans before 1923. Now is the time of trial predicted by Christ. Not all will be brave enough to endure the persecutions predicted by Christ, though great will be the reward for those who bring their white robes of Christian dignity "unstained into the everlasting life of Heaven."

Pope Francis has said, "Same-sex marriage is not simply a political struggle, but it is an attempt to destroy God's plan. It is a move of the 'father of lies' who seeks to confuse and deceive the children of God."[22] The president of the United States Conference of Catholic Bishops declared that the narrow vote of the Supreme Court "is a tragic error that harms the common good and most vulnerable among

[22] Edward Pentin, "Cardinal Bergoglio Hits Out at Same-Sex Marriage," *National Catholic Register*, July 8, 2010.

us."[23] Chesterton wrote in 1926: "The next great heresy is going to be simply an attack on morality, and especially on sexual morality." In 2008, Sister Lucia, who believed that she saw the Mother of Christ at Fatima, told Cardinal Caffarra: "The final confrontation between the Lord and Satan will be over family and marriage."[24] Injustice takes a harsh toll, but it cannot last, whereas "justice is eternal" (Wisd. 1:15).

I yield my column to some lines from the dissenting opinion of Justice Scalia, who is Catholic in practice as well as in name:

> A system of government that makes the People subordinate to a committee of nine unelected lawyers does not deserve to be called a democracy.... Four of the nine are natives of New York City.... The five Justices who compose today's majority are entirely comfortable concluding that every State violated the Constitution for all of the 135 years between the Fourteenth Amendment's ratification and Massachusetts' permitting of same-sex marriages in 2003. They have discovered in the Fourteenth Amendment a "fundamental right" overlooked by every person alive at the time of ratification, and almost everyone else in the time since.... The opinion is couched in a style that is as pretentious as its content is egotistic.... The Supreme Court of the United States has descended from the disciplined legal reasoning of John Marshall and Joseph Story to the mystical aphorisms of the fortune cookie.... With each decision of ours that takes from the People a question properly left to them—with each decision that is unabashedly based not on law, but on the "reasoned judgment" of a bare majority of this Court—we move one step closer to being reminded of our impotence.

July 5, 2015

[23] "Supreme Court Decision on Marriage 'A Tragic Error' Says President of Catholic Bishops' Conference," USCCB website, June 26, 2015.

[24] "Fatima Visionary Predicted 'Final Battle' Would Be Over Marriage, Family," Catholic News Agency, December 31, 2016, http://www.catholicnewsagency.com/.

Patriotism Begins in "Another Country"

The extended Independence Day weekend occasions some reflections on patriotism. The word is variously defined. Tolstoy called it an absolute vice, the essence of stupidity and immorality. In a famous essay in the 1980s, shortly after he converted to Catholicism, the Scottish philosopher Alasdair MacIntyre called it a central moral virtue. He drew on Augustine and Aquinas to shape his case:

> If I do not understand the enacted narrative of my own individual life as embedded in the history of my country ... I will not understand what I owe to others or what others owe to me, for what crimes of my nation I am bound to make reparation, for what benefits to my nation I am bound to feel gratitude. Understanding what is owed to and by me and understanding the history of the communities of which I am a part is ... one and the same thing.

Not long before St. Peter was crucified by a mad emperor, he had declared: "Honor all people. Love the brotherhood. Fear God. Honor the king" (1 Pet. 2:17). This is more than pragmatic politics. Like St. Peter, St. Thomas More got the order of obedience right, saying that he was "the King's good servant, but God's first." A true patriot would not think of honoring God as a mere ruler, nor fearing a mere ruler as God.

Just as there was an amazing explosion of artistic talent concentrated in Renaissance Italy, so too was the American Revolution a time of extraordinary acumen on display. George Washington had all the gifts needed to be a true Father of the Country. Alexander Hamilton put his unsurpassed genius to work in various ways of national service. Others knew the temptations of envy and venality but managed to subsume them under a higher cause.

Sometimes around July 4, I make a case for the widely misunderstood King George III, most recently in *Crisis Magazine*.[25] There still are people, unthinking thralls of cliché, who call him a "tyrant." A decade after the American Revolution, the king himself said that George Washington was "the greatest man in the world." Had they ever met, they would have enjoyed each other's company.

However one defines *patriotism*, Benjamin Franklin's words still obtain—to paraphrase: We have been given a republic, if we can keep it. The patriot's obligation to live a life of virtue is best kept by knowing the difference between earthly and heavenly cities. Thus the final stanza of Sir Cecil Spring-Rice's poem:

> And there's another country, I've heard of long ago,
> Most dear to them that love her, most great to them that
> know;
> We may not count her armies, we may not see her King;
> Her fortress is a faithful heart, her pride is suffering;
> And soul by soul and silently her shining bounds increase,
> And her ways are ways of gentleness, and all her paths are
> peace.

July 6, 2014

[25] Fr. George W. Rutler, "Born for Happiness and Misery: King George III," *Crisis Magazine*, June 30, 2014.

The Man for All Seasons

Our parish is blessed with a shrine to St. Thomas More. The young artist who painted the saint's image after Holbein was a refugee from communist Eastern Europe. He did such a good job that Cardinal Egan, dedicating it, said that he would not be surprised if this were the original.

We recently celebrated the joint feasts of St. Thomas More, who was chancellor of England, and St. John Fisher, bishop of Rochester. Their personalities were different in many ways, and it was almost a miracle that an Oxford man and a Cambridge man got on so well and eventually were canonized together. The Act of Succession and the Act of Supremacy were the challenges that King Henry VIII threw at them, and the saints returned the challenge. The issues were rooted in natural law: the meaning of marriage and the claims of government. These are the same issues that loom large today. Whatever our courts of law may decide about these matters, St. Thomas says: "I am not bound, my lord, to conform my conscience to the council of one realm against the General Council of Christendom." In 1919, in *A Turning Point in History*, G.K. Chesterton predicted with powerful precision that, great as More's witness was then, "he is not quite so important as he will be in a hundred years' time."

For every courageous saint back then, there were many other Catholics who instead took the safe path of complacency. More's own family begged him to find some loophole, and—after the sudden deaths of eight other bishops—Fisher was the only one left who acted like an apostle. Those who opted for comfort and wove the lies of their world into a simulation of truth had a banal and shallow faith that Pope Francis has called "rose water." It is a good image, for rose water is not blood and cannot wash away sin.

The "Man for All Seasons" wrote to his beloved Margaret from his cell in the Tower of London: "And, therefore, my own good daughter, do not let your mind be troubled over anything that shall happen to me in this world. Nothing can come but what God wills. And I am very sure that whatever that be, however bad it may seem, it shall indeed be the best."

The Fortnight for Freedom extended from the vigil of the feasts of Fisher and More to July 4, but its prayers continue, as the Church's many charitable and evangelical works are threatened by our present government's disdain for the religious conscience, most immediately evident in the Health and Human Services mandate[26] and the redefinition of marriage. In 1534 Henry VIII's arrogation of authority over the Church was quickly followed by a Treasons Act, which made it a high crime to criticize the king. In contemporary America as in Tudor England, the surest way to let that happen is to say, "It can't happen here."

July 7, 2013

[26] On July 2, 2013, in response to a national outcry from Catholic parishioners, clergy, and politicians, the appointed administrators of the Affordable Care Act (President Obama's federal takeover of medical care in the United States) made an "accommodation" to the stated moral objections that turned out to be no accommodation at all. The revised language still effectively ordered almost any employer—religious or secular—to violate Catholic morality by forcing employees to pay for group insurance coverage that included sterilization, abortion-inducing drugs, and contraception.

The Gift of Thunder

Jesus did not appoint the brothers James and John to be His apostles in spite of their tempers, but because of them. These *Boanerges* (Sons of Thunder) had wanted to bring fire down on the rude Samaritans. Jesus knew that such anger, if harnessed, could become "righteous." There is a difference between using temper and losing temper, as there is between oil for energy and the Gulf oil spill. Anger rightly used and not lost becomes strength. James became the first apostle to offer his life serenely for the Lord, and John in his maturity wrote, "Little children, love one another" (1 John 4:7).

The Risen Christ converted St. Paul's destructive wrath on the Damascus road. Later, the apostle would warn the Galatians that their uncontrolled temper was a "work of the flesh." St. Jerome's letters to St. Augustine show how hard it was for him to control his tongue and pen, and the sun often went down upon the wrath of the Irish missionary Columba. No saint, naturally placid or aggressive, replaced anger with the opposite extreme of timidity. "God has not given us a spirit of timidity, but a spirit of power and love and self-control" (2 Tim. 1:7).

The cure for both sinful anger and sinful timidity is the virtue of courage. St. John Chrysostom wrote to Theodore: "For if the wrath of God were a passion, one might well despair of being unable to quench the flame which he had kindled by so many evil doings; but since the Divine nature is passionless, even if He punishes, even if He takes vengeance, He does this not with wrath, but with tender care, and much loving-kindness; wherefore it behooves us to be of much good courage, and to trust in the power of repentance."[27]

Timidity disguised as charity can do more harm than anger. The conceit that evil will melt away by ignoring it would be like Captain Smith on the Titanic saying, "Iceberg? What iceberg?" St. Augustine said, "God does not need my lie." St. John Fisher, speaking as the only one of his country's bishops who was a true shepherd, lamented: "The fort is betrayed even of them that should have defended it." Four hundred years later, Churchill would say, "An appeaser is one who feeds a crocodile, hoping it will eat him last."

St. Alphonsus Liguori was not timid when he counseled: "Even when correcting faults, superiors should be kind." But his kindness was in fact the engine of his zeal to "admonish sinners," which is the first of the seven Spiritual Works of Mercy. Conversely, St. Leo confronting Attila the Hun, St. Joan of Arc trying to make a man of her pathetic king, and Blessed Jerzy Popieluszko staring down the Communists, were not foolhardy in their assertiveness. Their strength came not from Anger Management Therapy but from Christ, whose very wrath is merciful.

July 2, 2010

[27] St. John Chrysostom, *An Exhortation to Theodore after His Fall* 1, 4.

St. Benedict, the Prophet of Europe

In 1988 as Pope John Paul II began his speech to the European Parliament, Ian Paisley, a member for Northern Ireland, shouted that the Pope was the Antichrist. Another member, Archduke Otto von Hapsburg, seized him and, with the help of a few others, pushed him out of the hall. Since the archduke was the last crown prince of Austria-Hungary, it was as if a thousand years of popes and Holy Roman emperors had come alive again. In 2004, Otto had the joy of watching John Paul beatify his father, the Emperor Karl, in whose army the Pope's own father had devotedly served.

Shortly before his election to the papacy, Benedict XVI wrote a book entitled *Europe: Today and Tomorrow*. It was prophetic, and poignantly so, in light of the troubles that the European Union is having these days. The constitution of the Union studiously avoided mentioning the role of Christianity in the formation of Europe. The same Union has promoted many policies hostile to moral sanity, which have architected the structure of what successive popes have called a culture of death.

Hilaire Belloc said that "the Faith is Europe and Europe is the Faith." This could be a very limited and parochial view, but an expansive interpretation means that Europe would not be a triumph of civilization had it not been for the Christian sense of mankind. Europe cannot survive as a cohesive culture with a logical ground for its existence without Christianity as its animating force. This sense is lacking now, and the spiritual life of Europe, generally speaking, is materialistic and indolent, slothful about any transcendent perspective on life.

In 1980 Pope John Paul II named Sts. Cyril and Methodius, representatives of Eastern European Christianity, the Church's "other lung," co-patrons of Europe along with St. Benedict, whose feast we celebrate this week and whom Pope Paul VI proclaimed patron of Europe in 1964. In contrast to the functioning model for European unity—which seems to be, for the European Union, an entity bureaucratically sustained—St. Benedict preserved and promoted European culture through his carefully structured and maintained system of monastic confederations. This was not unlike, albeit in a supernatural order, the structure of fast-food chains or international corporations.

St. Benedict could once again be a unifier of Europe more effective than any bureaucracy in Strasbourg or Brussels. As he wrote in his Rule: "No one should follow what he considers to be good for himself, but rather what seems good for another. They should display brother love in a chaste manner, fear God in a spirit of love; revere their abbot with a genuine and submissive affection. Let them put Christ before all else, and may he lead us all to everlasting life."

July 10, 2016

The Best Things in the Worst Times

In our part of Manhattan there is no summer slowdown, and if there is demographic slack, any void is filled by the large number of tourists. The relentless pounding of steam hammers is an unnecessary reminder that our parish is in the midst of the biggest real-estate development in the history of the nation. We are part of that, as a spiritual animus and not as mere observers.

Stones and windows and marble in our present church came from the church of 1857. It was moved to build the Pennsylvania Station designed by McKim, Mead, and White, which was later destroyed by modern barbarians whose wrecking balls and dynamite are more potent than the axes and battering rams of the old Vandals and Huns. The sacrificial offerings of the poor parishioners built the best church they could. It never occurred to those who arrived on our docks as refugees to give God what remained after their ski vacations and summer cottages. The first parish school the immigrants built looked like a Parisian mansion, for they wanted the Faith taught to their children in petrine[28] tribute to Petrine[29] dogma.

The best intentions could not afford all the costs of the new church. The reredos behind the high altar remained unfinished until, over the past few months, we continued the work of polychroming. The increasing numbers of young people in the parish provided a pool of volunteers. And as God provides for us when we provide for God, various experts showed

28 "Made of stone."

29 That is, approved by the authority of St. Peter.

up unexpectedly to offer their help. My father liked to do gold-leafing as a hobby, and he taught me. I taught several others, who painstakingly accomplished much in at least eight hundred man-hours. One of our new parishioners lent scaffolding and several of the workers in his construction company—Ecuadoreans of singular craftsmanship and reverence. Our team represented more than half a dozen ethnic backgrounds united in the "one, holy, catholic" Faith, for the Church is universal in grace and thus is more than just international. A Jewish friend joined in. The work was finished in time for what would have been my own father's one hundredth birthday. Had he not already climbed the ladder that Jacob saw in a dream, I am sure he would have been up on the scaffold helping.

In our distressed nation, nothing is more essential than what barbarians consider unessential. I think of the youth who, in the days of Oliver Cromwell and his iconoclasts, built a church in defiance of a hostile government. He was imprisoned in the Tower of London and died at the age of twenty-seven. The tablet in his church in Leicestershire is inscribed:

> In the year 1653, when all things sacred were throughout the nation either demolished or profaned, Sir Robert Shirley, Baronet founded this church; whose singular praise it is to have done the best things in the worst times and hoped them in the most calamitous.

July 12, 2015

The Virtue of Patriotism

Popular myth has Martin Luther burning the *Summa Theologica* of St. Thomas Aquinas in the marketplace of Wittenberg. Not so. The hapless heretic wanted to destroy one of the world's greatest works, but none of the townsfolk was willing to surrender a copy. We should cherish Aquinas like that today, for he prevents a lot of pseudo-philosophical humbug.

In the month of Independence Day and Bastille Day, we recall that St. Thomas lists patriotism and piety as virtues under the governing virtue of justice. Patriotism gives the nation its due. The anarchist Emma Goldman called patriotism a superstition. Our Founding Fathers did not make the mistake of the French radicals who in 1789 denied God and His Church. One of the revolutionaries, Madame Jeanne Manon Philipon Roland, a founder of the Girondist party, learned that liberty running away from the judgment of God leads to terror. She went to the guillotine crying: "O Liberty, Liberty! What crimes are committed in thy name!"

Dr. Johnson called patriotism "the last refuge of a scoundrel." His friend and biographer, Boswell, explained that Johnson had not meant "a real and generous love of our own country, but that pretended patriotism which so many in all ages and countries, have made a cloak of self-interest." Camera-conscious politicians singing "Onward Christian Soldiers" (or refusing to do so out of political correctness) are not models of Aquinas's virtue of patriotism. Anyone can wrap himself in the flag and the cross, or demand a separation of the two, for self-promotion. The virtue is in those who offer their honor and lives for their fellow men.

God is God, whether or not we pledge ourselves to be one nation under Him. To unsay it is to deny that America is under divine judgment. George Washington took John Adams to a Catholic Mass in Philadelphia. These men of virtue, while not enjoying the fullness of the Catholic Faith, admired the Mass for its beauty and the sermon for its purity of moral doctrine. May the same be said of our own parish.

New York Harbor welcomed many immigrants. The book of Revelation shows another shore, where Heaven, our true native land, awaits. Our earthly home is worthy only as a sign of it. The Statue of Liberty is a civil icon of the Blessed Virgin, whose lamp is the light of Christ. Genuine liberty is the freedom from sin and death: "the glorious liberty of the sons of God" (Rom. 8:21). Washington wrote in his journal:

> O eternal and everlasting God, Direct my thought, words and work. Wash away my sins in the immaculate blood of the lamb, and purge my heart by thy Holy Spirit, from the dross of my natural corruption, that I may with more freedom of mind and liberty of will serve thee, the everlasting God, in righteousness and holiness this day, and all the days of my life.

July 14, 2002

Facing God

In 2014, Pope Francis appointed Cardinal Robert Sarah of Guinea to be Prefect of the Congregation for Divine Worship and the Discipline of the Sacraments, with instructions to continue a "reform of the reform."

After the Second Vatican Council, many changes in the liturgy were done virtually overnight, with no mandate from the Council, but motivated by what Pope Pius XII would have called a romantic "historicism" based on a mistaken understanding of the early Church's liturgy. Even some well-intentioned but misinformed Catholics have thought that inferior contemporary music and completely vernacular texts were the aim of Vatican II. A growing number of young Catholics understand better what the popes want for the liturgy than some aging people who have not outgrown the confusion of the 1960s and 1970s.

One change never mentioned by Vatican II was having the priest as a "presider" face the people all through the Mass. It came at a time when people were increasingly preoccupied with themselves, and it encouraged a psychology of self-absorption. The venerable *ad orientem* posture of the priest, always kept in the Eastern rites, is not a matter of his turning his back to the people. Rather, the priest faces East to direct the faithful's attention away from himself and toward the horizon symbolizing the Resurrection.

The readings and preaching (the *synaxis* or synagogue part) are done facing the people, for they are instructive, but the Holy Sacrifice (the *anaphora* or temple part) is offered with everyone facing in the same direction, rather than in what Pope Benedict XVI called an "enclosed circle." Pope Francis celebrates *ad orientem* in the Sistine Chapel. It has nothing to do with the placement of the altar, for the venerable manner—as in ancient basilicas—is a free-standing altar. In our own parish church, the *ad orientem* use is suitable for the altar in the nave as easily as at the older altar.

As Cardinal Sarah points out, liturgical innovations were supposed to invigorate Mass attendance, but they had the opposite effect, not to mention the countless millions of dollars spent on church renovations, which in too many cases ruined fine art. His Eminence has asked that parishes institute the *ad orientem* in the Ordinary Form by Advent, as a thing "good for the Church, good for our people." Actually, no permission is needed for that, since the original *General Instruction of the Roman Missal* left the position as a legitimate option, so it may be instituted at any time. The *ad orientem* use will be a modest change, different from the way innovations were made in the 1960s with tactless abruptness.

Cardinal Sarah said, "The liturgy is not about you and me. It is not where we celebrate our own identity or achievements or exalt or promote our own culture and local religious customs. The liturgy is first and foremost about God and what he has done for us."[30]

July 17, 2016

[30] Cardinal Robert Sarah, "Towards an Authentic Implementation of *Sacrosanctum Concilium*" (opening address to Sacra Liturgia, UK, July 5, 2016).

Pessimist or Optimist?

The pessimist and the optimist are much alike. Though the maxim has the pessimist seeing a glass half-empty and the optimist seeing it half-full, what they share is the confinement of their perspectives to the glass and what is in it. I'd rather be an optimist, because he tends to be more valiant.

King Saul with his spear was a pessimist who thought that Goliath was too big to be killed. David with his slingshot was an optimist who thought that the giant was too big to miss. But the attitudes of both were psychological. The morose personality sees threat, and the buoyant personality sees opportunity, but reality for both is only perception. It has been observed that the pessimist is an unhappy idiot and the optimist a happy idiot, for the self and the self's humor are the measure of all things.

There is agreement among both kinds of personalities that the world is going to end. Grimly or happily, they can cite physicists who expect that our planet will be finished by the year 500,000,000,000. But it will be too hot to sustain human life within a mere one billion years. These days, many seem to be pessimists who think that the world will end faster than expected, at least in terms of livable conditions affected by climate change. Some take this as a new gospel, and skeptics are treated as heretics facing an opprobrium as harsh as it is capricious, and as capricious as it is vicious. The argument is declared settled, even though no true science is ever settled.

No less a brain than that of Isaac Newton was confident that the world would end in 2060. The jury is still out on that. Now some Russian scientists complicate things by predicting that a 60 percent drop in solar activity will cause a mini ice age from 2030 to 2040, similar to the freeze from 1645 to 1715. We do know that Paul Ehrlich's book *The Population Bomb* predicted in 1968 that, long before now, four billion people would have starved to death, including sixty-five million in the United States. He continues to lecture to well-fed students at Stanford University.

Grigori Rasputin contaminated Russia with his pessimism, predicting that the world would end on August 23, 2013. That has happened only in places like Detroit. He was the opposite of P. G. Wodehouse's blithe Madeline Bassett, who thought that "the stars are God's daisy chain," and "every time a fairy blows its wee nose a baby is born."

The only settled science is that of the soul. It is neither pessimistic nor optimistic. It is the realism of Christ, who is the Eternal Logos, reason itself. Against pessimism and optimism it posits the virtue of hope. By hope, one trusts that God will grant eternal life and the means to attain it if one cooperates with the divine will, while recognizing the difficulties that lie in the path toward that blissful eternity. Hope has no patience for its dark enemy, pessimism, nor for its gossamer imitation, optimism.

July 19, 2015

Let Us Play

The vacation business is one of the biggest factors in the national economy—yet having a good time need not be expensive, if one understands what play really is. The best philosophers have long considered the human instinct for recreation. Such Catholic thinkers as Hugo Rahner and Josef Pieper have written whole books on *eutrepalia*, or recreation in relation to spiritual happiness. Catholicism considers the depth of the commandment to keep the Sabbath, understanding that we do not keep it right unless we associate the worship of God with enjoyment. Vacations in the summer and all enjoyable leisure reflect our relationship to God as His sons and daughters: as He delights in His creation, so should we.

Playfulness is a moral obligation. St. Thomas Aquinas calls playfulness one of the virtues allied with temperance, and he treats it under the virtue of *modestia*, which is moderation in outward movements. Playing games and telling jokes are virtuous because such playfulness gives rest to the tired soul, mind, and body. The great Doctor of the Church says that a lack of mirth or playfulness is a sin:

> In human affairs whatever is against reason is a sin. Now, it is against reason for a man to be burdensome to others, by offering no pleasure to others, and by hindering their enjoyment.... Now, a man who is without mirth not only is lacking playful speech, but is also burdensome to others, since he is deaf to the moderate mirth of others. Consequently they are vicious, and are said to be boorish.[31]

[31] St. Thomas Aquinas, *Summa Theologica*, II-II, Q. 168, art. 4.

Having fun must be moderate to be virtuous. The Christian parts with the modern pagan who desperately spends money and wastes time to find the happiness that can be found only in the love of God. St. Thomas says that our playfulness and entertainment (1) should not be indecent or injurious (i.e., it is wrong to have fun at the expense of others); (2) should not be out of balance (i.e., doing stupid and extravagant things "to have a good time"); and (3) should not be out of place (joking at funerals, acting silly at weddings, dressing slovenly in church, lacking respect for nature).

Happiness is more than a "happy hour." It is prelude to the happiness of Heaven. It demands that we see vacations, days off, attempts to find an hour's rest in a hectic day as clues that we are called to eternal happiness with God. The indiscreet joy of the saints has made this secret public. That is why we are never more at rest or happier than when we are with a saint.

July 28, 2002

An Accounting

My dear brothers and sisters in Christ,[32]

At noon on September 17, 2001, I became your pastor, and at noon on August 1 in this year of 2013 I relinquish that duty and move on to new work assigned to me by our cardinal. At the farewell gathering so splendidly hosted by you, I was shown photographs from many events in those years. Of them all, I was especially drawn to the one of me in a safety helmet and covered with dust on the day our city was attacked, and thousands were killed at the World Trade Center. Although I had not yet officially become pastor, I was in the process of moving in, and I was one of the many who were given water from canteens in front of our church. That beginning of my pastorate was in no metaphorical way a baptism by fire.

God, who brings good out of ill, has since blessed us in countless ways, but canon law does require some accounting. In those twelve years in our parish, 623 have been baptized into Christ, 433 have been united in holy matrimony, 79 have been blessed in death as they entered the larger life, and many others have been anointed in the hospitals.

Our Lord knows that 99 sheep are not enough if one more is lost. Since 2001 our flock has doubled, and there have been among them nearly a dozen who have been called to the priesthood. While I am the only priest in this parish, the visiting priests who assist in various ways

[32] This is Fr. Rutler's final letter to his parishioners at the Church of Our Saviour on Park Avenue in Manhattan before assuming his new position as pastor of the Church of St. Michael the Archangel on Manhattan's West Side.

have been a great support. I have heard in these twelve years possibly forty-five or fifty thousand confessions, and my fellow priests may have doubled that. No one save the angels in Heaven will know the wonderful graces that have been given in our confessionals, and that has been a chief joy to me, along with the priestly vocations of those fine young men who have been like sons to me.

Our small parish staff have always been loyal, and those who help in other ways have graciously preferred to go unnamed. The volunteer faculty of our CCD classes, which have grown tenfold, could more than match the finest of any school, and young people come from long distances for the Pre-Cana program, which is unsurpassed for its sound teaching of the joy of true marriage. The holy Liturgy has been accompanied year after year by our music director and choir. The men and boys who are our altar servers have instinctively and happily followed the directives of the Holy See, shunning theatrics and the clericalization of the laity by the misuse of Extraordinary Ministers of the Eucharist as though they were ordinary. During the week, I have been grateful for the service of Deacon Frank Orlando, who has recently been made director of formation for permanent deacons in the archdiocese. Our lectors read the sacred lessons of God's lively oracles with dignity and even cut short their ballgames and surfing in the summer to do so.

The good people of our parish, along with our extended family far and wide, have sacrificed to change the financial situation of this parish. Twelve years ago, we were burdened under millions of dollars of mortgage and other debts and costs for the repair of a building in which everything seemed to be collapsing at the same time. All that has been reversed, every penny of debt is paid, and the church has virtually been reconstructed, along with the installation of a new organ and many other improvements, renovations, and fine art. Our Lord was not fortunate in the one he chose to hold the moneybag, but the same Lord mercifully sent me trustees whose selfless devotion in these challenging years will bring them a reward more than I can give. There may have been times when my concern about the dire financial situation of our church made me seem, in the vernacular expression, cheap. Part of me is Scottish, a people known to practice thrift to a heroic degree, and in recent years I have even been made chaplain to our city's two leading Scottish societies. What once was owed is now matched by what is held in fixed funds for the maintenance of the church. The daily costs remain the responsibility of the people, in addition to our charitable and evangelical obligations, and I leave in the good hope that the results of the hard work of many will be preserved and stewardship will increase.

Perhaps someday, if I am permitted repose, I shall read into the record the lessons I have learned from people. That would not be an exercise in flattery or criticism, both of which are unworthy of a Christian, but it would be advice for our children when they are grown. When I became pastor of this parish, there were saints among us who guided me, and there were others who may become saints in a lengthier period beyond this world, but who did not make things easy for me. They were much tamer than Alexander the coppersmith (2 Tim. 4:14). I trust that in the future there will be no retreat to the old mistakes and abuses that have been addressed by our recent popes.

I have grown to love St. Paul more and more, and part of that is because, just as he tried to explain the gospel on Mars Hill in Athens, I have tried in a shamefully poorer way to do that here on Murray Hill in New York City. Since he is the saint that I am not, my only affinities with him are in his love of the Master, and his love for his people. That love was evident at Miletus, when he said farewell to the elders he had summoned from Ephesus as he was embarking for Jerusalem.

> And when he had spoke thus, he knelt down and prayed with them all. And they all wept and embraced Paul and kissed him, sorrowing most of all because of the word he had spoken, that they should see his face no more. And they brought him to the ship. (Acts 20:36–38)

I am only going to the far west side of Manhattan and not to Jerusalem, and you may see me from time to time; and instead of boarding a ship I may be on the Thirty-Fourth Street bus. But I do kneel like him as I leave, with happy tears of thanks for having been among you.

Faithfully yours in Our Saviour,

Fr. George W. Rutler
July 28, 2013

The Good, the Bad, the Ugly, and the Beautiful

One of my parishioners, now gone to the Lord, taught himself at least eight languages. This served Vernon A. Walters well in various important diplomatic roles and as a translator for presidents. Charles de Gaulle said, "Nixon, you gave a magnificent speech, but your interpreter was eloquent."

In a higher realm, something similar might be said of Silvanus, sometimes called Silas (1 Pet. 5:12). What Peter dictated was of the Holy Spirit, but Silvanus gave it a fine grammatical touch, and so we have some expressions as eloquent as they are immortal, like the "precious promises" by which "you might be partakers of the divine nature" (2 Pet. 1:4).

These words have to be understood carefully, lest they be twisted into some sort of Buddhist or Mormon confusion about humanity and divinity. "Deification" is a grant by God's will. St. Maximos (d. 662) said, "All that God is, except for an identity of being, one becomes when one is deified by grace." Peter, along with James and John, was perhaps not being deified at the moment he was dozing in the olive grove—while the Master prayed to His Father in His agony. But at the Last Supper that same evening, Our Lord had said: "I have given them the glory that you gave me, that they may be one as we are one—I in them and you in me—so that they may be brought to complete unity" (John 17:22–23). Peter had indeed seen this glory with the same sons of Zebedee on the mountain of the Transfiguration, which feast we celebrate this coming

Saturday. Christ had to explain to Peter the meaning of the divine light that had bewildered him.

That glorious occasion on the mountaintop was followed immediately by chaotic scenes at the mountain's base: a sick boy thrashing about and fierce words from Jesus about Satan. It is an instruction to us about life in the Church, for glimpses of glory are often followed, if not overshadowed, by suffering and sin. In my book *He Spoke to Us* there is a chapter called "The Transfiguration of the Church" because the Transfiguration of Christ is a lesson in the drama of the Church throughout history: the good, the bad, the beautiful, and the ugly are in tension, but they never blend into a mess. That is as true here in Hell's Kitchen in New York and in any neighborhood as it was in Galilee.

In the temporal life of the Church are some of the saddest disappointments precisely because the same Church is the home of the world's hope. Scandals and human failings are made more lurid in contrast to the sublime radiance that is the Church's bright gift to a dark world that otherwise would accept evil as the norm. No syntax of Silvanus could make more elegant the essence of the humble fisherman's astonishment: "We ourselves heard this voice from heaven while we were with him on the holy mountain" (2 Pet. 1:18).

July 31, 2016

“This Is My Glory”

Give me that old-time religion” goes the refrain of a catchy gospel hymn. The Catholic Church has the oldest memory—back to Eden—and it does not go into hibernation like Rip Van Winkle with the death of the last apostle, waking up only in the sixteenth century. We Americans have a rather loose grasp on what “old” means. A building just a hundred years old can expect to have a historic marker tacked on it. We can also forget that there is much of old America north and south of us.

The Pope refreshed our memory on July 30, when he canonized a lay brother in Guatemala. Pedro de San José Betancur was born in 1626 in Tenerife, Spain. The Massachusetts Bay Colony was taking root, the Ming Dynasty was in a civil war, Europe was torn by the Thirty Years' War, and the East India Company was establishing its commercial empire. In 1650 Pedro sailed to Cuba as a missionary. In 1651, the same year that Oliver Cromwell lamentably defeated the Scots, he went to Honduras and walked all the way to Santiago de los Caballeros in Guatemala.

Having failed in his studies for the priesthood, he made his profession as a Third Order Franciscan, and as a lay brother he worked as a gardener and a janitor. He bought a small house, which he converted into an oratory and an infirmary. Soon he founded the first school in Guatemala, a hospice for homeless men and women, and the world's first hospital specifically for convalescents. Until then, hospitals were basically hospices for the dying. The first native order in the New World, the Bethlehemites, took its name from the “Little House of Our Lady of Bethlehem,” which was the dedication of Betancur's oratory.

As Pope Clement XIV affirmed by declaring him Venerable in 1771, his good indicated sanctity, but he is a saint because of his practice to a heroic degree of the virtues theological (faith, hope, and love) and moral (prudence, justice, temperance, and fortitude).

Upon his arrival in Guatemala, Brother Pedro kissed the ground and said, "I must live and die here." Sixteen years later, at the age of forty-six, he looked at a statue of St. Joseph in his "Bethlehem Hospital" and died exclaiming, "This is my Glory."

It is a unique glory of the Catholic Church that she has saints. St. Pedro de San José Betancur's example helped convert the former Governor of Costa Rica, the Duke of Talamanca, who became Brother Rodrigo de la Cruz and took up where St. Pedro had left off. To postmodern Americans, all this was a long time ago. It was only about a quarter of the way back to the Resurrection. But the "old-time religion"—lived and renewed in the lives of the saints—is, in the words of St. Augustine, "ever ancient, ever new."

August 11, 2002

Confession Makes Us Worthy

When Our Lord offered to go to the house of the Roman centurion even though the man was not a Jew, the officer said, "I am not worthy to have you come under my roof" (Matt. 8:8). His words are remarkable because humility was not considered a virtue by the classical philosophers. The current translation in the liturgical text reads, "I am not worthy to receive you." A more accurate translation of the whole Mass is in the works, and I hope we have it soon.[33] The centurion's reference to his own house is especially to the point when the Blessed Sacrament is taken to the apartment of one who is ill. It always applies in church, for

[33] Another eight years would pass before the revised English translation of the Mass of Paul VI was released. The Latin had never changed from the wording in the traditional Latin Mass—which was based closely on the centurion's exclamation to Our Lord in Matthew 8:8: *Domine, non sum dignus ut intres sub tectum meum; sed tantum dic verbo, et sanabitur anima mea*, which, in the pre-1962 translation, with eighteenth-century usage, went: "Lord, I am not worthy that thou shouldst enter under my roof, but only say the word and my soul shall be healed." The revised translation we use in the pews today, finally released in Advent 2011 by the International Commission on English in the Liturgy, is dramatically superior to the rather limp summary Fr. Rutler cites from 2002. Similar to the pre-1962 translation, it is a vivid, specific, and powerful statement of this professional soldier's humility, his earnest respect for the customs of the holy nation occupied by his army, and his theologian-grade understanding of the miraculous powers of Jesus Christ, which he intuits are intended to heal not merely the Jews, but all men, and do not even require Our Lord's physical presence. Our souls, like the centurion's servant, are saved by the will of God.

however beautiful may be the building, the House of God is only a hint of the Everlasting Halls.

In the parable of the Two Debtors (Luke 7:36–50), a Pharisee named Simon invites Jesus to his house for a meal. Simon is unctuously polite, but there is none of the Roman's humility. He has the pose of a butterfly collector trying to pin down an exotic specimen. He calls Jesus "Rabbi" with the condescension of someone tolerating a deluded enthusiast. There is a tone of that sometimes when television interviewers invite a cleric on the show to discuss Church news.

A woman with a past shows up and is so deeply moved by Christ that she washes His feet with her tears and wipes them with her hair. The embarrassed Pharisee thinks to himself: "If this man were a prophet, he would have known who and what sort of woman this is who is touching him, for she is a sinner." Presumably, we know his private thought because he later made it public to justify himself. Jesus stirred his guilt: "Do you see this woman? I entered your house, you gave me no water for my feet.... You gave me no kiss.... You did not anoint my head with oil."

Jesus praised the righteousness of the Pharisees but not the self-righteousness of this Simon. Our self-righteous culture is quick to judge but slow to confess, because like the old pagan culture, it does not understand humility. It does not take seriously the sacrament of confession. It asks, as did the other guests under Simon's roof: "Who is this who even forgives sins?" There can be no renewal of the Church without renewal of confession. There is an increase in our parish, which is very good. We are not worthy, but every time we go to confession, we humbly receive Our Savior as He deserves to be received.

August 18, 2002

God's Blueprint

Our Lord was a construction worker. The Bible's word for carpenter can include various tasks: woodworking, stone cutting, blueprint-making, and bookkeeping. While Our Lord knew about Heaven, He also knew about contracting, and so He knew what He was talking about when He said that a man does not construct a tower without first estimating the cost (Luke 14:28).

I knew a priest, rather gruff on the surface, who wept at ordinations because he knew better than the young priests the cost of discipleship, and yet he loved the inestimable gift of the priesthood. The same thing happens at weddings when elderly couples weep, knowing the joy of the newlyweds but also the "richer and poorer, sickness and health" that ensues along the way to the serenity of golden age. Everyone smiles when a baby is baptized, but that lustral water inducts the child into the army of Christ, which, increasingly in our time, requires heroic sacrifice. Such is the price of glory.

Today we deeply grieve the fall of the Twin Towers. They were the costly marvel of their day. The banner in our church with the names of the firemen and citizens of our parish who died on September 11 recalls the unspeakable cost of living in a world attacked by evil. "Except the LORD build the house, they labor in vain that build it" (Ps. 127:1). We can never fail to praise the heroism of those who did great things that day, nor can we lament sufficiently the horrors inflicted by worshippers of false gods.

On a happy note, our parish in Hell's Kitchen, which has long known the challenges of crime and poverty, is the locus of the biggest building boom in the history of our nation. At each Mass we hear the sound of hammers through the stained-glass windows. The newest tower rising down the street will be 1,009 feet tall with corporate offices, condominium units, and a luxury hotel. Jesus the carpenter, who knows all things, knows that it involves a $2 billion capitalization, including $1.2 billion in debt. Our parish's debt is to the Lord for what we shall do for all the souls moving into this neighborhood. He shall demand from us an accounting.

St. Teresa of Calcutta knew that it would cost her much when she founded a religious order. Since then, many other religious orders have cut corners by selling out to worldly concerns, as though politically correct forms of "environmentalism" and "peace and justice" superseded the peace of Jesus and the justice of salvation. Some even abandoned their religious habits and communal lives. This is their last generation, as they resemble geriatric institutions. In contrast, Saint Teresa's Missionaries of Charity numbered twelve sisters in 1950. Today there are 5,161 sisters, 416 brothers, and 7,598 houses ministering to the poorest of the poor and bringing them the gospel. They counted the cost and have not labored in vain.

September 11, 2016

Politicians Playing Pope

The Roman consul Lucius Quinctius Cincinnatus (519–430 BC) was a model for our nation's Founding Fathers, who had no concept of a "career politician." Cincinnatus left his plough to serve his people and then returned to his farm when his work was done. Today there are many politicians who have had no career except public office. This can tempt them to think that power trumps truth. Recently, Archbishop Chaput said: "Catholic public leaders inconvenienced by the abortion debate tend to take a hard line in talking about the 'separation of Church and state.' But their idea of separation often seems to work one way. In fact, some officials also seem comfortable in the role of theologian. And that warrants some interest, not as a 'political' issue, but as a matter of accuracy and justice."[34]

Politicians who pick and choose the bits of Catholicism useful to their agenda are picturesquely called "cafeteria Catholics." There are, of course, moral principles that permit prudential disagreement, as with economic policy, war strategies, and capital punishment. Abortion is different, because its evil is intrinsic. Like Typhoid Mary early in the twentieth century, moral cafeterias can spread grave moral danger. It is safer to go with Blessed Mary than with Typhoid Mary. But the latter, who infected forty-seven people, only three of whom died, acted unwittingly. There are public figures

[34] Charles J. Chaput, "On the Separation of Sense and State," quoted in "Denver Archbishop Slams Pelosi on Church Teachings and Abortion," Catholic News Agency, August 25, 2008, http://www.catholicnewsagency.com/.

who willfully misrepresent Christ, and so they have His rebuke: "You are a hindrance to me; for you are not on the side of God, but of men" (Matt. 16:23). Ignorance is willful when it suppresses information. At the recent convention of one of our political parties in Denver, Archbishop Chaput was not invited to give an invocation, even though he is by far the most prominent religious leader in that area.

The Fourteenth Amendment remarks on the difference between a citizen and a person in its refutation of the *Dred Scott* decision, which, like *Roe* v. *Wade*, denied the human integrity of a person, not vouchsafed the rights of a citizen. The former denied the right to liberty, and the latter denied the right to life itself. The Lutheran theologian Dietrich Bonhoeffer, who was killed in the Flossenburg Concentration Camp, wrote in his *Ethics*: "Destruction of the embryo in the mother's womb is a violation of the right to live, which God has bestowed on this nascent life. To raise the question whether we are here concerned already with a human being or not is merely to confuse the issue. The simple fact is that God certainly intended to create a human being and that this nascent human being has been deliberately deprived of his life. And that is nothing but murder."[35]

If politicians want to campaign as "ardent Catholics," they should believe and act as ardent Catholics. As Archbishop Chaput has said from a pulpit better than any denied to him in the public forum: "If you're Catholic and you disagree with your Church, what do you do? You change your mind."

September 7, 2008

[35] Dietrich Bonhoeffer, *Ethics*, 175–176.

"We Have Become Too Proud to Pray"

As summer draws to a close, it seems that we have had very little of a lull in these weeks. Many of our parishioners have been on vacation, but a great many stayed in the city and were joined by an increasing number of tourists and visitors. The season reached a high point on Thursday, September 2, with a visit to our parish by the president of the United States, his father the former president, and their First Ladies. They joined me for some quiet time in the rectory followed by a prayer service in the church. The president is a man of sincere prayer and was intent on a Holy Hour for meditation. As this was to be private, no media or photographers and no public announcements were allowed until the actual day. The president and former president were joined in our church afterward by other officials, including the president's advisers, members of the cabinet and Congress, the governor and mayor and former mayor. It was not easy to maintain privacy with central Manhattan closed to traffic, hundreds of Secret Service and security, and armed guards on the church roof, but such is the protection required in these days of terrorism and confused people.

As we resume the normal pace of parish life, we note that 2005 will be the fiftieth anniversary of the chartering of the parish. In preparation, there are some worthy and exciting projects in store about which I will soon be writing. No parish responsible to Christ can be satisfied with itself as an enclosed "community," nor should its chief efforts be spent on the social entertainments of ourselves, although these are harmless and even helpful in due proportion. Our chief efforts must be in catechesis, spiritual formation, and evangelization. In such a time of challenge and growth, we should consider words written by Abraham Lincoln in 1863 and which I had the privilege of reading to our two presidential visitors and their guests:

> We have been the recipients of the choicest bounties of Heaven; we have been preserved these many years in peace and prosperity; we have grown in numbers, wealth and power as no other nation has ever grown. But we have forgotten God. We have forgotten the gracious hand which has preserved us in peace and multiplied and enriched and strengthened us, and we have vainly imagined, in the deceitfulness of our hearts, that all these blessings were produced by some superior wisdom and virtue of our own. Intoxicated with unbroken success, we have become too self-sufficient to feel the necessity of redeeming and preserving grace, too proud to pray to the God that made us. It behooves us, then, to humble ourselves before the offended Power, to confess our national sins and to pray for clemency and forgiveness.[36]

September 12, 2004

[36] Abraham Lincoln, "Proclamation Appointing a National Fast Day," Washington, DC, March 30, 1863.

The Exaltation of the Holy Cross

"We Sang a Dirge, and You Did Not Weep"

A friend sent me a collection of cartoons about the "smartphone" mania. Among the effects is the decay of the art of conversation. You can be reminded of this on busy Thirty-Fourth Street when people are so absorbed in "twittering" that they bump into you. One cartoon has figures of a bride and groom on top of a wedding cake, each fingering a smartphone, and another shows a crowd of people tweeting with one hand while holding in the other the sort of white cane that blind people use. Self-absorption is a form of moral blindness. Most poignant is the cartoon of a lonely little boy holding a soccer ball, totally ignored by other children staring at their smartphones.

The moral problem is antecedent to the computer age: "To what then shall I compare the men of this generation, and what are they like? They are like children who sit in the marketplace and call to one another, and they say, 'We played the flute for you, and you did not dance; we sang a dirge, and you did not weep'" (Luke 7:31–32).

Our Lord made those remarks in the context of criticisms against Him, citing the fickleness of His accusers, who resented the way He exposed the limitations of their self-absorption. For others without the audacity to challenge Him, it was sufficient to ignore Him. An ancient lament was a prophecy of Christ's timeless reproach to those too preoccupied with themselves to pay Him attention as He hung on the Cross, whether in the first century or in the computer age: "Is it nothing to you, all you who pass by? Look and see if there is any sorrow like my sorrow" (Lam. 1:12).

But for those who stay alert and look beyond themselves, September 14 celebrates the Triumph of the Cross. In the eighth century, a boy in Syria was born mute but found his voice the day he received Holy Communion at the age of seven. He apparently loved to sing from then on, and St. Andrew of Crete now is known as a hymnographer, as well as a bishop and a theologian. He explained why the Cross takes us out of ourselves:

"Had there been no Cross, Christ could not have been crucified. Had there been no Cross, life itself could not have been nailed to the tree. And if life had not been nailed to it, there would be no streams of immortality pouring from Christ's side, blood and water for the world's cleansing. The legal bond of our sin would not be cancelled, we should not have attained our freedom, we should not have enjoyed the fruit of the tree of life, and the gates of paradise would not stand open. Had there been no Cross, death would not have been trodden underfoot, nor hell despoiled."[37]

September 13, 2015

[37] St. Andrew of Crete, homily on the Exaltation of the Cross.

I Shall Hold You Responsible

On the feast of the Exaltation of the Holy Cross, the Church rejoices in the mercy of Our Lord, who suffered such a cruel death for our salvation. Mercy moved Christ to condemn most vigorously those who harm innocent life. Abortion is the defining moral issue of our age, as slavery was in the nineteenth century. In our country, the lives destroyed by abortion each day outnumber all combat deaths in war over the last ten years.

Although the bishops corrected the Speaker of the House of Representatives in her misrepresentation of the Church's teaching on life in the womb, she has persisted in her inaccuracies. On network television on September 7, one of the vice-presidential candidates repeated the same misinformation, even though he has been prevented by his bishop from speaking on church property because of his misstatements. For the record, the United States Conference of Catholic Bishops has published the facts:

1. From earliest times, Christians distanced themselves from pagan cultures by rejecting abortion and infanticide, as is evident in the New Testament, the "Didache" and "Epistle of Barnabas" and regional Church councils. The prophet Jeremiah (1:15) declared of God: "Before I formed you in the womb, I knew you." And the last and greatest of the prophets, John the Baptist, greeted Our Lord while still in his mother's womb.

2. While the time of "ensoulment" in the womb was discussed by theologians such as Augustine, often referring to the writing of Aristotle and pre-Christian philosophers who had no

knowledge of the existence of the human ovum, all of these theologians affirmed the Church's common conviction that life itself begins at conception and that abortion is gravely wrong at every stage.

3. Penalties for abortion often varied according to the stage of gestation, but abortion has always been seen as a grave moral evil from the moment of conception.

4. Modern genetics has demonstrated that the union of sperm and egg at conception produces a new living being that is distinct from both mother and father. From the mid-nineteenth century, all obsolete distinctions between the "ensouled" and "unensouled" fetus were permanently removed from canon law.

Politicians who relegate the facts of life to the category of religious views rather than natural law ignore physical science; and they violate the traditional separation of church and state when they twist Christian moral teaching in the civic forum. The Church is patient with ignorance, but not with willful ignorance. Civil and religious leaders are equally accountable to the injunction of the prophet Ezekiel (33:8):

> If I tell the wicked, "O wicked one, you shall surely die," and you do not speak out to dissuade the wicked from his way, the wicked shall die for his guilt, but I will hold you responsible for his death.

September 14, 2008

"Why Are You Silent?"

I do not like most jargon, as it diminishes the creative power of the noble English language rightly used. For instance, I do not like to be told by bureaucratic sorts to "prioritize." (Apparently, the first recorded instance of its use was in the 1972 presidential campaign.) As with all things, Christ the Living Word put it better when He said, "But seek first the kingdom of God and his righteousness, and all these things will be added to you" (Matt. 6:33). God and His promise of eternal life should have priority over every other desire or concern.

Recently, many television viewers complained about a news bulletin covering the beheading of the journalist and devout Catholic James Foley. Their objection was not to the horror of the news but that it had interrupted the broadcast of a soap opera. We are learning quickly that people with that defective kind of priority will soon find out the hard way that life is not a soap opera. We are now engaged in a war, whether or not some politicians hesitate to call it that, and it must have priority over all other interests. The war is being fought by enemies of God, deluded by the conceit that they are fighting for God.

This is so hard for an indulged and selfish culture to accept, inasmuch as it means acknowledging that good and evil exist, though many would prefer to ignore the latter. Christians are being martyred in the Middle East, and public officials still find it hard to mention that those who are being crucified, beheaded, and driven from their homes are suffering because they are Christians.

The auxiliary bishop of Baghdad, Shlemon Warduni, said on Vatican radio: "We have to ask the world: Why are you silent? Why do not you speak out? Do human rights exist, or not? And if they exist, where are they? There are many, many cases that should arouse the conscience of the whole world: Where is Europe? Where is America?" The genocide of Christians, who have been in Iraq since shortly after the Resurrection, does not seem to have priority in the attention of many in our country.

As this suffering continues, many in the United States are willing to tolerate heresy and moral decadence in a vain attempt to "get along" with others. While Christians must "love the sinner and hate the sin," there are an increasing number of people who are intimidated into enabling the sinner to advertise his sin. In 1992, Cardinal O'Connor said that compromising Catholic truth for the sake of political correctness was "not worth one comma in the Apostles' Creed."[38]

The holy martyrs in the Middle East honor the Church and atone for our degeneracy. Their bishops are willing to struggle and die with them. They must be amazed that bishops and people in other places have their priorities so wrong.

September 14, 2014

[38] Quoted in Francis X. Clines, "Irish March Up the Avenue, Gay Protesters at Bay," *New York Times*, March 18, 1993, http://www.nytimes.com/.

"Without the Lord's Day, We Cannot Live!"

While Advent begins the liturgical year, and January 1 starts the new civil year, September is the beginning of what constitutes most of the daily order of life, from schools to courts. There really is no slow season in the parish: while many quit the neighborhood for other parts, many tourists take their place. As the regular parish calendar resumes, with our educational programs now stretching the physical resources of the church building (some reconfiguring of space in the undercroft and installation of new computers are helping our expanded enrollment), we are especially thankful for the many ways in which our people are volunteering in various capacities. As both a measure of our spiritual life and a promise for the future, our baptisms are well more than twice their number just five years ago. While August is a relatively slow-paced month for weddings, eleven couples will wed in this month of September, and all of them will have had sound instruction.

Our special prayers go up for the three young men who have so faithfully served at our altar and now are by God's grace preparing for the sacred priesthood. Vincent Druding is well advanced in the seminary course. Peter Heasley has begun studies in the Neumann Residence of the seminary. James Platania has begun his studies at Mount St. Mary's Seminary in Maryland for the Diocese of Paterson, where his family lives. It may be rare or unprecedented for a parish to have helped nurture three seminarians at the same time, and I know that among our parish's obligations there will be a particular regard for helping them in every way. New times teach new duties, and these challenging times call for special vigor in Christ's priest. In *The Imitation of Christ* Thomas à Kempis writes: "A priest clad in his sacred vestments is Christ's vicegerent, to pray to God for himself, and for all the people, in a suppliant and humble manner."

During his recent apostolic visit to Austria, Pope Benedict XVI preached something that is a most important reminder for all people in every parish at the start of a new season:

> "*Sine dominico non possumus!*" Without the gift of the Lord, without the Lord's day, we cannot live: That was the answer given in the year 304 by Christians from Abitene in present-day Tunisia, when they were caught celebrating the forbidden Sunday Eucharist and brought before the judge. They were asked why they were celebrating the Christian Sunday Eucharist, even though they knew it was a capital offense.... For these Christians, the Sunday Eucharist was not a commandment, but an inner necessity. Without Him who sustains our lives with His love, life itself is empty. To do without or to betray this focus would deprive life of its very foundation, would take away its inner dignity and beauty.[39]

September 16, 2007

[39] Benedict XVI, homily at St. Stephen's Cathedral, Vienna, September 9, 2007.

The Opening

Our parish is blessed with many musicians, some of whom you may recognize from the concert halls and opera, and others who visit when they are in the city. I am two handshakes from Puccini, because his granddaughter introduced herself to me after Mass one day. That greatest violinist Fritz Kreisler (1875–1962) grew up in Vienna in a musical home that Brahms occasionally visited, and he studied under Bruckner and Massenet as a child prodigy. His father was physician to Sigmund Freud, who couldn't understand why the boy wanted to be a musician. That little boy shook all those hands. Bishop Fulton Sheen, who often assisted and preached here, received Kreisler and his wife, Harriet, into the Church. Shortly before he died, Kreisler lost his sight and hearing in an automobile accident. Bishop Sheen said that in his dying days Kreisler "radiated a gentleness and refinement not unlike his music."[40]

There is a story that Kreisler saved his money as a young man to buy a fine violin, only to find that it had already been sold to a wealthy collector of musical instruments, who kept it in a locked cabinet. The man refused to sell it, although he could not play it himself, but he let Kreisler play it to see how it sounded. The collector was so moved that the instrument could "sing" that he let Kreisler have it. By the end of Kreisler's life, in addition to his beloved Vuillaume violin, which was his constant "second fiddle," he owned several Stradivari, Guarneri, and Bergonzi violins, almost all named for him. The tale of the collector is sometimes told of

[40] *Treasure in Clay: The Autobiography of Fulton J. Sheen* (New York: Image, 1980), 270.

others, but the point has universal application as a parable of ourselves. We exist, but we come fully alive only through God's grace, and when Christ enters the soul, it is like being taken out of a locked cabinet and being able to sing. This is the portent of St. Irenaeus of Lyons' assertion: "The glory of God is man fully alive." And, by the way, on a more exalted plane than my two handshakes from Puccini, Irenaeus was two handshakes from the Apostle John, who saw the Risen Lord.

That Lord once told a deaf man, "Ephphatha" (Mark 7:34). Pope Benedict XVI has said:

> This little word, *Ephphatha*—"Be opened"—sums up Christ's entire mission. He became man so that man, made inwardly deaf and dumb by sin, would become able to hear the voice of God, the voice of love speaking to his heart, and learn to speak in the language of love, to communicate with God and with others. For this reason, the word and the gesture of *Ephphatha* are included in the Rite of Baptism, as one of the signs that explain its meaning: the priest touching the mouth and ears of the newly baptized says: "*Ephphatha*," praying that they may soon hear the Word of God and profess the Faith.

September 16, 2012

Calling for Faith

On Friday, September 8, it being the occasion of my twenty-fifth anniversary, I wore the cassock in which I was ordained. I have recounted to some of you how I was being fitted for it in the tailor shop of Signore Gammarelli when Pope John Paul II was shot, the sound of the gun echoing in the square. Since then, that cassock has seen many events. It is a symbol of the dramatic events that have taken place in the years I have so far been privileged to serve as a priest. It is not possible adequately to express my gratitude for the remarkable celebration of my anniversary on the feast of the Nativity of the Blessed Mother. I have never seen such a wonderful gathering of people in our church or heard such joyful singing. The reception afterward stretched the capacity of our undercroft beyond legal limits, but no one complained. It is humbling to be able to thank all those who worked so hard to offer such a transporting act of worship and conviviality. It was a magnificent way to begin our return from the summer months. I extend my deepest thanks for all the kindnesses and generous expressions from people in the parish, our beloved city, and so many countries, all witnessing to the breadth of our holy Church.

This Sunday, September 17, precisely at noon, marks the fifth anniversary of the canonical start of my office as pastor of this parish. Like the twenty-five years of my priesthood, these five years in the parish have seen momentous events. I took up my responsibilities when the air was acrid from the attack on the World Trade Center. For many of our new parishioners and visitors it is hard to imagine the challenges we faced then. While much more needs to be done, I am deeply grateful to the loving power of the Holy Spirit, who has given strength to preserve what was worthy, mend what was broken, guide the wandering, encourage the perplexed, reprove the obdurate, and raise up new life. In all this there was the heroic witness of John Paul II and Benedict XVI to lead us. Many things I urged upon my arrival as pastor as necessary elements of authentic renewal and Catholic witness are being realized on a global scale by our Pope, whose writings influenced me greatly many years ago. I pray that God's grace will help me to become a better pastor day by day, and always to be faithful to the promise I made at my installation five years ago:

> With firm faith I also believe everything contained in God's Word, written or handed down in tradition and proposed by the Church, whether by way of solemn judgment or through the ordinary and universal magisterium, as divinely revealed and calling for faith.[41]

September 17, 2006

[41] Congregation for the Doctrine of Faith, Profession of Faith.

A God Who Scandalizes

A certain kind of journalism thrives on scandals, but they are not what a theologian or any kind of deep thinker means by a scandal. A skandalon is a stick in a trap that ensnares an animal that touches it. Intellectually, it is a mental trap on the path to truth. St. Paul said that the concept of God becoming human in Christ was a kind of joke for the Greek philosophers, who enjoyed playing with words—but for the Jews, to whom God had first revealed Himself as singular and lofty, it was scandalous to the ultimate degree. The philosophers in Athens smirked, but the rabbis in Jerusalem beat their breasts in anguish.

The *scandal of particularity*, which has challenged theologians, is the fact that the immeasurable Creator of the Universe is concerned with the minutest details of His creation, to the extent that He both dwells in Eternity and also is born as a man in His own created time and space. But a related scandal is this: each human being is of huge value to God, so much so that He dies to unite each one of us to Him.

Some serious theologians without the gift of faith might react to this with a shudder, like the ancient rabbis. Others who do not believe in God at all simply dismiss the idea with a flick of the hand. For them, the only value of a man is what he can produce for the benefit of others, be it scientific or artistic, or just cleaning windows and digging coal. In that calculus, an individual is worth a fraction of a crowd and counts only as part of a mob. If an unborn baby is inconvenient to his mother, he may be aborted, and if an elderly lady finds it hard to climb stairs or remember who she is, she may be euthanized.

Unclear thinkers of our day who call themselves "spiritual but not religions" want a God who is an amorphous vapor, making no demands of them and merely justifying their animal passions and providing background music when they look at a sunset. That sorry misuse of the imagination will never understand why Jesus looks for the lost sheep and embraces the prodigal son who has tired of living like a pig.

How many people Josef Stalin killed is debated. Solzhenitsyn figured it was about sixty million, but a generally accepted figure according to one calculation is "only twenty million." Jesus never spoke of "only one lost sheep." Neither would he agree with Stalin that "one death is a tragedy; one thousand is a statistic." In our culture, the proposition that each human life is of infinite value scandalizes, but it also is the substance of our faith in the Word made flesh. "You were bought at a price" (1 Cor. 6:20).

September 18, 2016

Grace Confronts Evil

Last Sunday I joined various city officials in dedicating the block of East Fortieth Street in front of Engine Company 21 to Captain William Burke, who gave his life on September 11, 2001. The parish provided the chairs from our undercroft for the crowd that gathered. The men of our firehouse did all the work in setting up the chairs, and expressed their gratitude. This is humbling, since all of us are honored by being able to show in such small ways our gratitude for the sacrifices of our firefighters, and to the wives and children left to mourn those fallen heroes.

The war against terrorism engages everyone in various ways. The shocking events of September 11 taught our nation that we are no longer able to enjoy isolation from the sufferings caused by malignant people driven by hate. The unspeakable torture and slaughter of hundreds of children recently in Russia was more evidence of the viciousness that marks the enemies of basic human dignity.[42]

For several generations, it has been the fashion to deny the reality of good and evil, and to reduce human behavior to a pragmatic, naturalist calculus of psychological adjustment or maladjustment. But once

[42] On September 1, 2004, Muslim terrorists from the Russian province of Chechnya attacked a Russian school in nearby Beslan in North Ossetia and took hostage about 1,000 people, mostly children. Over three days of largely futile negotiations, the terrorists murdered more than 300 of the hostages, including 186 children. Russian special forces finally blew down a wall of the gymnasium where the surviving hostages were being held and evacuated them—and then used tanks and flamethrowers to eliminate the remaining terrorists.

you shun God and stop believing in the existence of supernatural evil, holiness and villainy seem incomprehensible. Added to their political motives, this helps to explain why so many journalists shrink from identifying terrorists as terrorists. With remarkable consistency, our major news services have called those who massacred the Russian children in Beslan virtually everything except evil. Only slightly less remarkable than the term "activists" (*Pakistan Times*) are these euphemisms: "hostage-takers" (*Los Angeles Times*), "fighters" (*Washington Post*), "commandos" (*Agence France-Presse*), "radicals" (*BBC*), "separatists" (*Christian Science Monitor*), and "insurgents" (*New York Times*).

Jesus never hid behind euphemisms when He confronted evil. He not only told the truth; He is the Truth. The Christian must expose what the morally shy would conceal: the present horrors that fill the landscape with innocent victims are caused by the rejection of Jesus Christ as Lord and Savior. Economic and political complexities are precisely that: complications. But the radical *cause* of terror is not complicated. It is the denial of the Truth of God. Man did not invent evil, but man is accountable for not converting souls to the Truth—as the Living Truth Himself commanded us to do as He ascended to the right hand of His Father.

Our Lord wills that each of His children be born at a certain time in history. He has honored us by giving us life in this season of the human drama, and we must honor Him by bringing souls to conversion. The essential dynamic for this is the grace that daily converts our own hearts and minds.

September 19, 2004

God Calls

Today, Pope Benedict XVI declares John Henry Newman "Blessed," which means that it is "worthy of belief" that this singularly numinous figure of the nineteenth century is in Heaven and able to intercede on behalf of those who invoke him in prayer. Beatification is the third act in the fourfold process of canonization. The final declaration of sanctity, declaring that the saint enjoys the Beatific Vision, universalizes devotion to the saint. Like Blessed Teresa of Calcutta, Newman already has a wide circle of devotees.

This beatification is of historic importance in a double way. First, Pope Benedict XVI is personally declaring the Formula of Beatification during his state visit to the United Kingdom. It is the first time that the Holy Father has himself performed a beatification, and he does so because of the influence Newman had on his life. Secondly, while a feast day customarily marks the *dies natalis*, or day of death and birth into Heaven, the Pope is choosing as Newman's feast day October 9, the day on which he was received into the Catholic Church in 1845 by the Passionist priest Dominic Barberi, who also is a Blessed. Newman is presented to the Church as a convert who embraced the fullness of the Faith after a long struggle of mind and heart. He would write:

> For us Catholics, my brethren, while we clearly recognize how things are going with our countrymen, and while we would not accelerate the march of infidelity if we could help it, yet we are more desirous that you [Anglicans] should leave a false church for the true, than that a false church should hold its ground. For if

> we are blessed in converting any of you, we are effecting a direct, unequivocal, and substantial benefit, which outweighs all points of expedience—the salvation of your souls.[43]

While we anticipate our dedication of a shrine to Newman on September 23, it is fitting that this exemplary priest should be honored today when we pray for those preparing for the priesthood and offer a special collection for St. Joseph's Seminary. Our parish is graced with many vocations. Last year our parishioner Father Druding celebrated his first Mass here. We now have four more young men in seminary, and several are in the process of spiritual discernment.

Everyone has a vocation to holiness, according to one's state in life. Like the prodigal son, whose life was changed when he decided to return to the house of his father, so are we summoned each day to a new conversion of intellect and will. This week we shall be singing several hymns written by Newman, and among them is a line he wrote during a severe fever on board a ship, which was also a moment of crisis in his life: "I do not ask to see the distant scene; one step enough for me."[44]

September 19, 2010

[43] John Henry Newman, *Lectures on Certain Difficulties Felt by Anglicans in Submitting to the Catholic Church* (1850), quoted in Edward T. Oakes, "Newman on Conversion," *First Things*, February 13, 2008, https://www.firstthings.com/.

[44] From "Lead, Kindly Light."

The Time We Are Given

The return of activities after the summer lull reminds one of St. Augustine's description of the Christian life as "ever ancient, ever new." The unchanging truths of God are refreshed with every renewal of the calendar. The city has its own attractions in the summer, and visitors from quieter places sometimes are surprised when I call New York a ghost town in August. While I spent this summer in Manhattan, I was able to accept an invitation to London last week, where I marked my ordination anniversary in Westminster Cathedral at a High Mass for the organization Aid to the Church in Need, with His Beatitude Fouad Twal, Patriarch of Jerusalem. It was a reminder of the universal personality of the Catholic Church, encompassing time as well as geography. The Patriarch can trace his diocese back to the apostle James the Less.

While ancient pious cartographers placed Jerusalem at the epicenter of the world, there are those today who put New York there, and there are even those who more specifically locate the center in Murray Hill. The fact is, our location is important, as the many special gatherings of diverse organizations, especially in this season, indicate. For instance, we have just hosted a special Mass for a national association for the blind, and for several days a group of Irish bishops on the board of Maynooth College have said Mass here. This Thursday Archbishop Dolan will say the Red Mass here for the Catholic judges and attorneys of the archdiocese, and at the same time the president of Guatemala will attend a reception in our undercroft. The next day we will host a Vigil for various bishops and knights and dames of the Order of the Holy Sepulchre, and there will be various baptisms and weddings as well. We are accountable for taking advantage of the time we are given on earth to promote the gospel.

Cardinal Spellman had his critics when he erected our parish, for they thought the neighborhood did not need another church, and that its prospects were not promising. The vicissitudes of subsequent years and the practical difficulties in building and maintaining our church have not overwhelmed the wonderful fruition of the gifts of the Holy Spirit here. As Pope Benedict XVI has declared this the Year for Priests, so might we locally call this the Year for the Parish as we celebrate the fiftieth anniversary of the solemn blessing of our church building. In recent years, with the mortgage debt paid, the church was solemnly dedicated and the bulk of our restoration work was completed. This year should be a time to rededicate ourselves to the great work entrusted to us. May our simple but fervent celebration of our first fifty years on October 8 inspire all of us to heights higher than the hill on which our church stands.

September 20, 2009

Christians Persecuted in the Lands of the Bible

A parish is particularly privileged when the Pope comes not only to its city, but to the parish itself. Our church has one of the largest capacities in the archdiocese, and we will be hosting a special Holy Hour this Thursday for nearly a thousand young adults. Madison Square Garden will be the site of the Pontifical Mass on Friday, for reasons of sheer size and security. On a building on Eighth Avenue, two minutes from our church, is a fine mural that took 100 gallons of paint to show a welcoming figure of Pope Francis, 225 feet high and 93 feet across. This work was the contribution of the Diocese of Brooklyn and will remain in place as a reminder of his visit for six weeks after the Pope departs New York for the major part of his U.S. visit in Philadelphia.

One urgent pastoral matter that Pope Francis has been addressing as the Chief Shepherd of his flock is the refugee crisis in Europe, but it also affects us. There are probably as many opinions on how to deal with this as there are people trying to form a cogent response, but especially prudent is the counsel of bishops in places such as Hungary and Slovakia who know from long experience the consequences of confusing naïveté with mercy. Ninety percent of the current refugees are Muslim, and the situation is complicated by the fact that ISIS boasts that there are many of their own people among them. The founder of Nasarean.org, Father Benedict Kiely, has noted: "Emotion, rather than a rational response to a real problem, seems to be the guiding light for the panicked reaction of so many world leaders."[45] To their shame, the very rich Islamic states in the Persian Gulf have not accepted a single refugee.

A bipartisan resolution introduced in Congress calls the persecution of Christians in that sorry part of the world "genocide." This past year, 120,000 Christians were driven from the Nineveh Plain in Iraq with no possessions. During more than four years of civil war, the ancient Christian community in Syria is being destroyed. Christians are not a significant part of the immigrant tide flooding Europe from the UN camps in Syria, Jordan, and Turkey because Islamic terrorists have driven them out of those camps for refusing to convert. A Hungarian bishop rightly insisted, and was criticized for it, that to most of the migrants, Christians are second-class citizens. Europe and our own administration in Washington are virtually ignoring their plight, refusing to acknowledge that their Christian faith is the essential fact in the calculus of their suffering. When Coptic Christians were slain in Egypt, our government avoided calling them anything other than "Egyptian citizens."[46] As Father Kiely has said, "Political correctness is not only a new form of totalitarianism, it is dangerous to national security."[47]

September 20, 2015

[45] Fr. Benedict Kiely, "Unchristian Refugee Policies," *FaithZette*, February 5, 2016, http://www.lifezette.com/.

[46] This column dates from the last eighteen months of the Obama administration.

[47] Kiely, "Unchristian Refugee Policies."

Hints of Heaven, or Hell

Catholicism has long distinguished itself from Puritanism in its joyful embrace of feasts and recreation. But while Puritanism disdained forms of entertainment basically because they were entertaining, the Church has been cautious of the tendency of entertainment to degrade instead of edify. For a long time, pipe organs that worked by water pressure were banned from the Liturgy because such instruments supplied background music for the martyrdoms of Christians in the Colosseum and the Circus Maximus.

Politicians have long known how to exploit entertainment. The Lincoln-Douglas debates were highly amusing, with Douglas at five feet four inches matching himself against Lincoln at nearly six feet four inches. Whiskey flowed freely. Douglas orated in deep and sonorous voice in contrast to Lincoln's curiously high tenor. Both were honorable men and took each other and the crowd seriously. Douglas, whose wife and sons were Catholic, resisted the bigotry of the Know Nothing Party and willed his estate for the foundation of the University of Chicago. In this instance entertainment was to good effect.

The Roman satirist Juvenal (55–127) knew the dangers of weak-willed people being manipulated by demagogues through mindless public spectacles. He described the decay of republican Rome into the decadence of the later imperial era when the Caesars bought support by offering *panem et circenses*, lamenting that "the people that once bestowed commands, consulships, legions, and all else, now meddles no more and longs eagerly for just two things—bread and circuses."[48]

[48] Juvenal, *Satires* X, 78.

Ignoring the lesson that should have been learned from the Munich Olympics of 1936, staged to divert the world from the Nazi crimes, the media and business interests recently indulged the Beijing Olympics, expressing minor irritation at reminders that one and a half million people had been dispossessed to build the Olympic center, and that political prisoners were suffering while the crowds watched a spectacle that outdid the choreography of Speer. On the closing day of the games, while the medalists were being honored, the seventy-three-year-old bishop of Zhengding, Julius Jia Zhiguo, was arrested for leading underground Catholics in celebrating the feast of the Assumption. He will most likely not be paid millions of dollars to endorse products on television.

Anyone who had not watched television for the last generation would find it hard to believe what passes for entertainment on the screen today: the coarse language, degrading acts, and numbing banality. Classical philosophers connected legitimate pleasure with virtue: *id quod visum placet*, or "that which pleases." They did not mean that any amusement is good. The expression means what pleases a man indicates his character. A beautiful soul is drawn to beautiful things. What makes us smile should be a hint of Heaven. Gratification only on the animal level is a glimpse of the opposite. George Bernard Shaw said that Hell is a place where the only thing you have to do is amuse yourself.

September 21, 2008

Apocalypse

It is my opinion as I write this on the evening of September 15 that the world will not end tonight.[49] If you are able to read this on the following Sunday, you will know that I was right. If I am wrong, nothing made of matter really matters anymore. That is the whole point to thinking about the end of the world, or *apocalypse*—from the Greek ἀποκάλυψις (*apocalypsis*) or "uncovering." Every material consideration, concern, obsession, and distraction will vanish when all creation is subsumed into the Creator, so that God will be "all in all" (1 Cor. 15:28). All will be "uncovered" or revealed.

Our Lord warned that speculation about the end times is futile. He knew that there would be fanatics and demagogues stirring the crowds with claims that the end is just around the corner. We should not go "running after them" (Luke 17:23). False evangelists find that sort of thing good for business (though I suspect they invest some of their donations in long-term Treasury bonds). But Dr. Billy Graham, a far more estimable representative of the Evangelical school, says it is hard not to think that we may be approaching the end of the world when we see all the terrible portents these days. Pope Francis has not declared the end of the world, but he has said that it seems we are moving piece by piece toward World

[49] Texas televangelist John Hagee published a book in 2013 and subsequently created a series of online video specials suggesting that, given the upcoming occurrence of four lunar eclipses or "blood moons" beginning April 14, 2014, the world would end on September 15, 2015. The blood moons occurred on schedule, but as of this writing, the world has not yet ended.

War III. Given technology, such a conflict could be hard to distinguish from the consummation of all that is, at least on this planet.

Secular thinkers may mock apocalyptic theology, but they have indulged their own versions of it in dire predictions of economic disaster (recall the Y2K hysteria of 2000) and global warming/cooling/change (or whatever may be its current *nom du jour*). There may be substance to some of these speculations, but it is unscientific of scientists to treat a hypothesis as a conclusion. When they do, ecology becomes its own theology, and anyone who disagrees is a heretic. And if everything were to begin melting or freezing, one senses that anticipation of the End will be a cause not of reverence, but of anxiety. An atheist is less likely to cry, "Come, Lord Jesus!" than to moan, "Oh my God!!"

Jesus says, "Be not anxious about tomorrow" (Matt. 6:34), because He is in control. Without him, we are out of control. As William Butler Yeats wrote in "The Second Coming":

> Things fall apart; the centre cannot hold;
> Mere anarchy is loosed upon the world,
> The blood-dimmed tide is loosed, and everywhere
> The ceremony of innocence is drowned;
> The best lack all conviction, while the worst
> Are full of passionate intensity.

When things seem to be spinning out of control, just look to Jesus on the Cross. There is the love that made the world and that will bring it back to Him. *Stat crux dum volvitur orbis*. "The Cross is steady while the world is turning."

September 21, 2014

Prayers for Peace — Not Pacifism

The church was filled with people all day long on September 11, sometimes out into the street—lighting candles, going to confession, and attending one of the six Masses. Our local Engine Company 21 used some of our tables and chairs for their open house for mourners and friends. A helmet representing the late Captain Burke rested in state in front of the Paschal candle in silent witness to the toll taken at the World Trade Center.

In heroic acts of last year, we saw the great good of which the human race is capable, and a culture that had grown banal in its awareness of evil saw its horror directly. One of our parishioners tells of a macabre coincidence by which a neighbor in her apartment building lost a son in one of the airplanes and a daughter in the other, and of another neighbor who left a wife and small child. She also tells of the trauma still endured by a little girl who saw a couple plummeting hand in hand past the window of her school.

War must always be the last resort, but it can be a legitimate resort, and, indeed, the Doctors of the Church teach that it can be a sin not to fight to protect justice and innocence against enemies who intend destruction. Retribution is not revenge, and selfless vindication is different from selfish vindictiveness.

While we are obliged to forgive our enemies, forgiveness requires an act of contrition from the guilty. Glibly to forgive without requiring a conversion of heart is what a theologian and victim of the Nazis called "cheap grace."[50] It is sentimentality, and sentimentality is love without

[50] See Dietrich Bonhoeffer (1906–1945), *The Cost of Discipleship* (1937). Bonhoeffer, a young pastor in a Protestant denomination called the

sacrifice. Christ Crucified hangs at the crossroads of history as the ultimate sign of that. We are baptized into Him whose parables in various ways offer mercy for the repentant sinner and eternal punishment for those who consort with evil. "If thy brother trespass against thee, rebuke him; and if he repent, forgive him. And if he trespass against thee seven times in a day, and seven times in a day turn again to thee, saying I repent: thou shalt forgive him" (Luke 17:3–4). Those who speak as though forgiveness were cheap and undemanding, and who find it comforting that the New Testament rarely mentions Hell, skirt the uncomfortable fact that in those rare instances the speaker is Christ.

Our nation's leaders have heavy responsibilities, as do the members of our armed forces and our allies who are prepared to risk their lives for us. They must be high in our prayers, even as we continue to pray that there may be peace among nations.

September 22, 2002

Confessing Church, was a heroic preacher, organizer, and spy who worked tirelessly in the German resistance to Nazi rule. He was arrested in 1943 and executed on April 9, 1945 in Germany's Flossenbürg concentration camp, two weeks before American infantry divisions arrived to liberate it.

The Times — Yet to Change

Last week, Pope Benedict XVI was in Lebanon, where the principal Catholic rite, the Maronite, traces its roots to St. Maroun, who in the fourth century was a friend of St. John Chrysostom. The Holy Father spoke to people who "know all too well the tragedy of conflict and ... the cry of the widow and the orphan."

Like Blessed Teresa of Calcutta, the Pope linked violence to contempt for the right to life: "The effectiveness of our commitment to peace depends on our understanding of human life." The defense of life "leads us to reject not only war and terrorism, but every assault on innocent human life, on men and women as creatures willed by God. Wherever the truth of human nature is ignored or denied, it becomes impossible to respect that grammar which is the natural law inscribed in the human heart."[51]

This contradicts those in our own country who plead for peace while violating the innocent unborn. Our current president has defended partial-birth abortion. In opposing the Born-Alive Infants Protection Act of 2002, he infelicitously put it, "fetus, or child—however way you want to describe it—is now outside the womb."[52]

It is not surprising that the *New York Times* should be so opposed to the Catholic Church, whose teaching on the sanctity of life exposes the hypocrisy of that publication. If, according to the adage, "hypocrisy is the

[51] Benedict XVI, address at May 25th Hall of the Baabda Presidential Palace, September 15, 2012.

[52] John Jalsevac, "Unearthed Audio: Obama Calls Newborn Baby a 'Fetus outside of the Womb,'" Lifesite News, August 24, 2012, https://www.lifesitenews.com/.

tribute which vice pays to virtue," there is much vice promoted by the *New York Times*. But one is hard-pressed to detect the remnant virtue.

Pope Benedict's final Mass in Lebanon attracted 350,000 people, and yet the largest gathering of faithful in the long history of that ancient land was mentioned only on the bottom of page 8 of the *New York Times* with a tiny photograph. The same issue's "Quotation of the Day" was from an "Egyptian religious scholar," Ismail Mohamed: "We don't think that depictions of the prophets are freedom of expression; we think it is an offense against our rights." This is where hypocrisy burst into a veritable tap dance, for in March of this year, the *Times* ran a full-page advertisement mocking the Catholic Church and, a few days later, refused to run a similar one mocking Islam.

The "Grey Lady" is only a few shades removed from what Our Lord called "whitewashed tombs." The mainstream media have defended vulgar and even pornographic anti-Christian films, stage plays, sculptures, and painting, referring to them as "art" entitled by free expression. Yet when it comes to Islam, there is a different standard. Perhaps it is because newspaper editors know that Pope Benedict XVI will not demand that they be decapitated.

The Pope risked his life to go to the Middle East. At eighty-five, he still is on active duty. And so will be his successors, long after the last subscriber to the *New York Times* has cancelled his subscription.

September 23, 2012

God Is Not Pleased by Blood

Many in the communications media, accustomed to sound bites, lack the ability to follow the reasoning of Pope Benedict XVI's brilliant lecture at the University of Regensburg. Some journalists misrepresented him, inciting fanatics who burned churches and killed, and threaten worse to come. The *New York Times*, which defends films and art blaspheming Christ, demands that the Pope apologize to hysterical holdovers from the Bronze Age. Among the words excised from most reports of the lecture were those of the Byzantine emperor Manuel II Palaeologus: "God is not pleased by blood, and not acting reasonably is contrary to God's nature.... Whoever would lead someone to faith needs the ability to speak well and to reason properly, without violence or threats."

The Pope's lecture includes lines taken verbatim from part II, chapter 2 of his book *Truth and Tolerance*, which we have been selling in our parish bookstall this past year, and which caused little comment until demagogues distorted it.

The *Times* of London, to its credit, commented in a September 17 editorial that the Pope wanted to show the contradiction between religion and holy war. "Violent conversion to any religious faith, or for that matter violent oppression of religious opponents, goes against God's Nature." One immediately thinks of journalists kidnapped and ordered to convert to Islam at the point of a gun. Reaction to the Pope's lecture shows that a large number of Muslims are not interested in rational debate. The Holy Father was insulted, burned in effigy, and threatened. It was an unfortunate sequel to demonstrations after the publication of

Danish cartoons critical of Mohammed, which led to the massacre of more than one hundred innocent people.

Our civilization is at stake. They are naïve who think that fanatics are not serious in their malice. Mr. Chamberlain thought Hitler might be reasoned with as a gentleman. After the Yalta Conference, President Roosevelt opined that under the surface Stalin might be "a Christian gentleman." Countless millions died because of those miscalculations.

Last Sunday, the city authorities assigned police protection to our own parish because of feared violence from Islamic extremists demonstrating nearby. If God assigns particular people to be His witnesses in each age, we should feel honored that He had us conceived in this generation, to witness to His gospel with reason and charity.

The London *Times* said, "The clash of civilizations is not between Christianity and Islam. It is between those who favor open debate and those who think free speech is anathema.... The Vatican has said [the Pope] is very sorry his speech caused such offence to Muslims. That is fine but it should not go further than that.... As in the case of the Danish cartoons, Muslim zealots are trying to impose their restrictions of free expression on the West. Mindful as we should be of religious sensitivities, that cannot be allowed to happen."

September 24, 2006

Terrorism and Using Our Brains

Egyptian embalmers assumed that the brain would not be needed in the afterlife, and so they threw it away. Since there will be no need for sun or moon in the Heavenly City, for "the Lamb is the lamp thereof" (Rev. 21:23), the "glorified body" may enjoy immediate perception. But God expects us to use our brains in this temporal world. Jesus did not commend the dishonesty of the unjust steward (Luke 16:1–12), but He said we should use our minds as justly as the steward did unjustly.

The human brain is the most complex machine in the universe, with eighty-six billion neurons. The Johns Hopkins neurologist Barry Gordon refuted the myth that people on average use only 10 percent of the brain's capacity. Although at rest the brain uses just a small fraction of its capacity, even then it is using around 20 percent of the body's energy, while making up only about 3 percent of the body's weight.

The Catholic Faith is not a form of brainlessness. It needs reason to avoid superstition, just as reason needs faith to avoid rationalism. So Pope St. Pius X asserted in his *Oath Against Modernism*, "to be sworn to by all clergy,... religious superiors ... and professors," that "faith is not a blind sentiment of religion welling up from the depths of the subconscious under the impulse of the heart and the motion of a will trained to morality; but faith is a genuine assent of the intellect to truth received by hearing from an external source." The first Bishop of Rome said that Christians must use their brains: "Always be ready to give a defense to everyone who asks you a reason for the hope that is in you" (1 Pet. 3:15).

Étienne Gilson wrote: "We are told that it is faith which constructed the cathedrals of the Middle Ages. Without doubt, but faith would have constructed nothing at all if there had not also been architects; and if it is true that the façade of Notre Dame of Paris is a yearning of the soul toward God, that does not prevent its being also a geometrical work. It is necessary to know geometry in order to construct a façade which may be an act of love."[53]

Within a ten-minute walk of our church in these past few days, one man attacked an officer with a meat cleaver, and another man planted two explosives. The first man had shouted Islamic slogans outside a Brooklyn synagogue in July and was declared "not a terrorist threat." The human brain can rationalize unreality if it replaces true faith in God with its own agenda. In 1899 William Hughes Mearns wrote about a ghost:

> Yesterday, upon the stair,
> I met a man who wasn't there.
> He wasn't there again today,
> I wish, I wish he'd go away.

Terrorists are not ghosts and will not go away even if reasonably intelligent people misuse their brains to pretend they are not there.

September 25, 2016

[53] Étienne Gilson, "Intelligence in the Service of Christ," in *Christianity and Philosophy* (1936).

The World Is Dying to Hear It

In this month the Church prays for vocations. The past generation saw a drastic drop in vocations to the priesthood and religious life. Now there seems to be a resurgence, not in little measure encouraged by Pope Benedict's example of classic theological and liturgical integrity.

St. Joseph's Seminary in Yonkers is welcoming a class larger than any in recent years, distinguished by the high quality of candidates. St. Paul's Seminary in Minnesota has its largest enrollment since 1981. St. Cloud's is the largest in more than forty years. In Maryland, Mount St. Mary's Seminary has 163 seminarians.

Among religious communities, the Dominican Sisters of Mary, Mother of the Eucharist, a teaching order founded only in 1997 with four sisters, now has a community of 113. The Nashville Dominicans have admitted the largest number of postulants in 150 years. Among the orders for men, the Dominican Province of St. Joseph, which includes New York, this year accepted its largest novitiate class since 1966. Archbishop Augustine Di Noia, a member of that Province, has said:

> Our tradition is constituted by a unique convergence of qualities: optimism about the rationality and fundamental goodness of the natural order; an abiding certitude that divine grace and mercy are sheer gifts, unmerited and otherwise unattainable; a healthy realism about the peril of the human condition apart from this grace and mercy; a determination to maintain a God's-eye view of everything that exists and everything that happens; an appreciation of the inner intelligibility of everything that God has

> revealed about himself and us; a wholly admirable resistance to all purely moralistic accounts of the Catholic faith; . . . a zealous willingness to preach and teach about all this, in season and out, because we are convinced that the world is dying to hear it and dying from not hearing it.[54]

Everyone has a vocation by virtue of Baptism, be it in the lay state, clerical, consecrated religious, married or single, young or old. The newly beatified John Henry Newman prayed:

> God has created me to do Him some definite service; He has committed some work to me which He has not committed to another. I have my mission — I never may know it in this life, but I shall be told it in the next. Somehow I am necessary for His purposes, as necessary in my place as an Archangel in his — if, indeed, I fail, He can raise another, as He could make the stones children of Abraham. Yet I have a part in this great work; I am a link in a chain, a bond of connection between persons. He has not created me for naught. I shall do good, I shall do His work; I shall be an angel of peace, a preacher of truth in my own place, while not intending it, if I do but keep His commandments and serve Him in my calling.

September 26, 2010

[54] Quoted in "Why Are Young People Being Attracted to the Dominican Order in Such Numbers?" website of the Cambridge Lay Dominicans, October 12, 2013, http://laydominicanscambridge.blogspot.com/.

A Sign of the Renovation of Our Souls

The Solemn Blessing of our parish church by Cardinal Spellman took place exactly fifty years ago on September 27. By happy circumstance, that date this year is a Sunday. The church could not be consecrated to the Lord at that time, since construction debts still obtained. In recent times the mortgage was paid, and Cardinal Egan was able to dedicate it officially to Our Savior as a gift of the faithful. So now we are entrusted with the care of this beautiful building, remembering that the structure is only stones, but the mystical Church is made up of the faithful who gather here to pray in union with the saints and angels who attend every Mass.

The visible witness of the church building is, nonetheless, a sign of Christ's presence here in the middle of Manhattan. "The stones of the wall will cry out, and the beams of the woodwork will echo it" (Hab. 2:11). Those words were brought to the highest pitch when Our Savior entered Jerusalem to die for us (Luke 19:40).

Christ loved the Temple in Jerusalem and regularly returned to His Father's House. He drove out those who were defiling it and predicted that it would be destroyed and rebuilt. The latter promise, of course, referred to Himself, for the earthly structure is a symbol of Christ's own body. Faithful Christians must constantly purify God's House spiritually through honest prayer and true worship, just as they have to keep it in repair physically. Recent years, as so often in history, have seen abuses of true religion. Those challenges have elicited the noble words of modern popes calling for a renewal and strengthening of the faith once delivered to the saints. "Zeal for my Father's house has consumed me" (John 2:17).

The ongoing work of preserving and adding to the art in our church, for which we thank so many of our talented parishioners who are giving of their time so generously, is an outward sign of the constant renovation of our souls by the Holy Spirit, who makes all things new (Rev. 21:5). Our God does not make all new things, which would be mere novelty, but He renews the life first endowed to us, in preparation for eternal life. This is why the church is a holy house and not a museum.

While the ongoing celebration of our fiftieth anniversary will include Solemn Vespers and Benediction of the Blessed Sacrament on Thursday, October 8, we will make a special act of thanksgiving this Sunday, recalling the words of the seventh-century hymn "Angularis fundamentum":

To this temple, where we call thee,
Come O Lord of Hosts today;
With thy wonted loving kindness,
Hear thy servants as they pray.
And thy fullest benediction,
Shed within its walls alway.

September 27, 2009

The Front Lines

Our Holy Father offered Holy Mass this past Friday practically next door in Madison Square Garden. Next Thursday, October 1, one of our parishioners, John Wilson, will be ordained to the diaconate in St. Peter's Basilica in Rome along with forty others. He will be the only New Yorker among them, and, while I shall not be there, Cardinal Dolan will be the ordaining prelate. We look forward, God willing, to John's priestly ordination next May and his first Mass here at St. Michael's. I have been blessed to assist a long line of candidates for Holy Orders and am grateful that the abundance of priestly vocations is now evident here at St. Michael's, which has had a venerable history of producing young priests—for many years in abeyance, but flourishing again. Also, this week we celebrate our patronal feast with a Triduum beginning Sunday evening and culminating on the Tuesday feast, assisted by a large number of Haitians who customarily fill our large church in veneration of the patron of their native land.

All this is taking place in what has long been called Hell's Kitchen. It is riveting to think that the successor of Peter has been in Hell's Kitchen, and that young men here are now taking up the call to spiritual combat in this time of severe cultural confusion and threats to the Holy Church in many manifestations, civil and moral.

Perhaps it was a singular inspiration in 1857 that chose St. Michael the Archangel as our patron. Who better to cast out evil? Against all those who mock and disparage the Faith of the saints, he wields a mighty sword—much like the one convincingly depicted on our statue of him in the church, and also in the painting over the chimneypiece of the rectory dining room.

Quis ut Deus? That is the Latin for Michael, which in Hebrew means "Who is like God?" The answer is no one or no thing: no civil executive, or judge, or congressman is like God. And no one can change the truth of God, try as they sometimes might.

Now that Hell's Kitchen is becoming the most valuable real-estate development in our nation's history, it risks falling prey to the temptations of affluence, which could be worse than the old afflictions of crime and vice born of poverty. I am glad there has been strong resistance among merchants and residents to "gentrifying" Hell's Kitchen by renaming it Clinton. Even if the eponym were the noble Governor DeWitt Clinton, whose picture used to be on the $1,000 bill, since replaced by Salmon P. Chase (not that I have ever seen one in our Sunday collection), it is better that we enjoy the old name, since in spiritual combat it means that we are on the front line, like Octavian's Actium or Wellington's Waterloo.

September 27, 2015

Bodies and Bullet Holes

To bury the dead is one of the seven corporal works of mercy. The human body is to be treated with respect from conception through death. In the general resurrection of the dead, the body will be glorified in a mysterious way in union with the soul. The Church regulates the treatment of the dead (CCC 2000). Burial of the body is normative, but cremation is permitted, provided that it does not signal disbelief in the resurrection of the body. In a large city, with cemeteries often far removed, it is still desirable that the body of the deceased be brought to the church for the funeral Mass before burial or cremation. Only by exception is a body to be cremated before the funeral and the ashes brought to the Mass. I am occasionally surprised when people are uninformed about these things and make funeral arrangements before consulting a priest.

A Manichean concept of the body virtually worships it as an idol in life and then treats it as irrelevant after it has lost its earthly usefulness. Contempt for God leads to contempt for the human body. At the South Street Seaport, there currently is a display of 22 whole bodies and more than 260 additional organs and partial body specimens. "Bodies—The Exhibition" is a version of "Body Worlds," which in recent years has exploited prurience in the name of scientific edification. The corpses are skinned, and the blood replaced with silicon polymers. These plasticized bodies are shown in various poses, sometimes whimsically. Dr. Thomas Hibbs, professor of ethics and culture at Baylor University, has called it pornographic.

The founder of "Body Worlds" is Gunther von Hagens, who invented the "Plastination" method at the University of Heidelberg. He is not culpable for his father having served in the Nazi SS in a perverse age when lampshades were made of human skin. That horrified people then. A generation later, more than twenty million people around the world have paid to view "plastinated corpses" for the thrill of it. In 1996, von Hagens moved to China, where bodies were more easily obtainable, some of them rumored to be the bodies of homeless or mentally ill people or executed prisoners. In 2004, bullet holes were found in two of the exhibited "sculptures." The anonymous bodies on display in Manhattan were taken from the Dalian Medical University in northern China. The New York State legislature this summer passed a bill requiring a declaration of the cause of death of the exhibited remains. Is it possible that if you visited this exhibition, you were looking at a Christian martyr?

"Do you not know that your body is a temple of the Holy Spirit, who is in you, whom you have received from God? You are not your own; you were bought at a price. Therefore honor God with your body" (1 Cor. 6:19–20).

September 28, 2008

Never Lose Heart

In the liturgical readings these days, as in much of the past summer, our Lord teaches through parables. Since there are twenty-four of them, it would be possible to spend almost half of all the Sundays of the year preaching on the parables alone. Unlike stories told by mortal men using plots and images to reach up to lofty heights, Our Lord uses parables to reach down from the heights of Heaven itself. After all, He came down from and knows all about it, because that is His home, and in this world He had no permanent dwelling place. Our stories about Heaven are speculation; His are information.

As Christ knows the heights, in a system of contradictions He likewise knows the depths. He knows the ways of Satan better than we do, just as Satan knows the ways of God better than we know them, and Jesus tells parable after parable to encourage us, because He knows that the essential strategy of Satan is to discourage. Now, to discourage is to remove the heart. And Satan wants us to lose heart in order to make us share in his heartlessness.

There are times in the human annals, and in every individual life, when men and their methods face discouragement. So it was in the fourteenth century when the Scots set out on crusade to rescue the Holy Sepulchre from the Moors. Robert the Bruce, declared the legitimate king of Scotland by Pope John XXII, had died in 1329 asking that his embalmed heart be carried with the army to the Church of the Holy Sepulchre. Sir James Douglas carried the heart with his troops on the journey to Jerusalem, in a silver and enameled box hung around his neck. In Granada, Douglas encouraged the troops by flinging the heart ahead of them and, according to one version, shouting: "Now pass thou onward as thou wert wont, and Douglas will follow thee or die." The army was defeated by the Muslim foe, but the heart of King Robert was found on the battlefield, along with the body of Douglas, and taken back to Scotland and buried under the high altar of Melrose Abbey.

The heart of Jesus is not embalmed and is never lost. He encourages His Church, in spite of the failings of her human members, both clergy and lay. In the parable of the Two Sons, one son promises to serve his father and does not, while the other refuses, but in the end does his father's bidding. The point is that cynical professions of intent fail, but those who are honest, even to the extent of saying they will not serve God, can channel that honesty into obedience. So Our Lord encourages each of us: Do not be disheartened. Try your best, but be honest.

September 28, 2014

Sophia Institute

Sophia Institute is a nonprofit institution that seeks to nurture the spiritual, moral, and cultural life of souls and to spread the Gospel of Christ in conformity with the authentic teachings of the Roman Catholic Church.

Sophia Institute Press fulfills this mission by offering translations, reprints, and new publications that afford readers a rich source of the enduring wisdom of mankind.

Sophia Institute also operates two popular online Catholic resources: CrisisMagazine.com and CatholicExchange.com.

Crisis Magazine provides insightful cultural analysis that arms readers with the arguments necessary for navigating the ideological and theological minefields of the day. *Catholic Exchange* provides world news from a Catholic perspective as well as daily devotionals and articles that will help you to grow in holiness and live a life consistent with the teachings of the Church.

In 2013, Sophia Institute launched Sophia Institute for Teachers to renew and rebuild Catholic culture through service to Catholic education. With the goal of nurturing the spiritual, moral, and cultural life of souls, and an abiding respect for the role and work of teachers, we strive to provide materials and programs that are at once enlightening to the mind and ennobling to the heart; faithful and complete, as well as useful and practical.

Sophia Institute gratefully recognizes the Solidarity Association for preserving and encouraging the growth of our apostolate over the course of many years. Without their generous and timely support, this book would not be in your hands.

www.SophiaInstitute.com
www.CatholicExchange.com
www.CrisisMagazine.com
www.SophiaInstituteforTeachers.org

Sophia Institute Press® is a registered trademark of Sophia Institute.
Sophia Institute is a tax-exempt institution as defined by the Internal Revenue Code, Section 501(c)(3). Tax I.D. 22-2548708.